KANYE WEST SUPERSTAR

BYRON CRAWFORD

COPYRIGHT © 2014 BYRON CRAWFORD
ALL RIGHTS RESERVED.
ISBN-10: 1500586188
ISBN-13: 978-1500586188

For Kendall Jenner

"Sometimes people write novels and they just be so wordy and so self-absorbed.
I am not a fan of books.
I would never want a book's autograph.
I am a proud non-reader of books."

– KANYE WEST

CON7ENTS

1. A Big, Bright, Shining Star 1
2. You Didn't Build That 15
3. I Gave You Fair Warning 27
4. George Bush Doesn't Care About Black People 40
5. We Don't Mess with Dark Butts or Lace Fronts 52
6. Must Be This Tall To Ride 63
7. Show Some Courtesy, Curtis 75
8. Upgrade U 86
9. There's No Easy Way Out 98
10. I'mma Let You Finish (Nullus) 110
11. One Less Lonely Dreaded N-Word 125
12. Ray J Hit It First 135
13. Yeezus H. Tapdancing Christ 147

BYRON CRAWFORD

BYRON CRAWFORD

ACKNOWLEDGEMENTS

The author wishes to thank the makers of Bud Ice and Pabst Blue Ribbon, both of which were on sale while he was working on this; Theotis Jones a/k/a the hardest working man in show business; Dan Auerbach of The Black Keys, for the shout-out in The New York Times; the people who copped his first four books, i.e. his enablers; his parents, for pretending to not notice when food went missing, 15 years now into his adulthood; and the lovely ladies of RackRadar, for giving him a reason to get out of bed in the morning other than fear of utter financial ruin.

BYRON CRAWFORD

1
A Big, Bright, Shining Star

I like prōn as much as any healthy, red-blooded Murican man, maybe even more so, but not so much that I would marry a prōn chick.

Sure, if my career as an author of reasonably-priced hip-hop ebooks takes off to the point where I have the means, or if I found one who was down on her luck and I had some meth on me, I would make sweet, passionate love to a prōn chick. There's several of them I would like to make sweet, passionate love to, and in fact, I'm already putting together a list, just in case. But I'd have to draw the line at marriage.

I wouldn't want a prōn chick to be my child's mother, both because I wouldn't want him to grow up to be messed up in the head – like Hugh Hefner's son, who's alleged to have beaten up one of the Playmates – and because I want both of his parents to be intelligent, not just the father. I figure I'm already bringing a lot of bad genes into the equation, transferred via reproductive material that may have been damaged from years of hard living. It doesn't seem as viscous as it once was.

And really, I wouldn't want a prōn chick in my house while I'm not at home, and I'm sure it would be awkward – to say the least – to try to get her to not be in the house when I'm not there, especially if we're married. She might not like the idea of having her own separate Airstream trailer on the premises, like the one Andy Dick lives in, in his baby's mother's backyard. All prōn chicks have pimps that they turn over the $300 they make per scene to, and as revealed in the documentary-like film Casino, they don't lose touch with those pimps just because they got married.

Kanye West is not as concerned with whether or not something seems like a good idea. He's the kind of person who will accomplish anything and everything he sets his mind to, regardless of what other people think. That's the essence of who he is both as an artist and as a person. On the one hand, this has led him to become one of the most successful rappers of all time, of ALL TIME, despite the fact that he's not a very good rapper, and on the other hand it's led his personal life to become an increasingly ridonkulous public spectacle.

We'll be discussing both in this book – probably the tabloid aspect of his life more so than his artistry, but definitely his artistry as well. Because if it weren't for his artistry – to the extent that you can call it that – there wouldn't be a tabloid aspect of his life to speak of. Kim Kardashian is not interested in megalomaniacs who simply sit around in their mom's basement ranting and raving on the Internets. Otherwise, I probably would have been in line somewhere behind Ray J and ahead of Kanye.

Before she was off the market, but definitely not the first.

Born in Atlanta, Georgia, in the year of our lord 1977, Kanye West moved with his mom to Chicago as a young child. His father stayed put in Atlanta, where Kanye would sometimes visit during the summer and may have picked up some of his bad taste in music. Later, his father relocated to Maryland, where he became a marriage counselor in a church.

I'm not sure what led to the dissolution of his relationship with Kanye's mother. I really would have asked her (I have her email address), but she's been dead since 2007. The fact that Kanye's father was once a marriage counselor in a church makes me suspect that he's an epic manwhore, and that would help explain Kanye's obsession with pron. Guys with a few failed marriages under their belt pursue marriage counseling as a career because they've had a lot of experience being in relationships; and it's a well-known fact that guys who are in leadership positions in a church get a lot of pussy thrown at them by female parishioners.

If I actually believed anything that was ever said in a church, and if attractive women went to black churches (I don't know if a black man can become a leader of a white church, which is probably for the best), I might consider becoming a leader of a church myself, if only to have a system in which pussy is delivered to me, so I wouldn't have to sweat trying to procure it by some other means.

Ever since I read an article by Malcolm Gladwell in the New Yorker about Jerry Sandusky bufuing those kids at Penn State, and later some guy told me a method this guy on his job uses (I probably shouldn't be any more specific than that, though this wasn't illegal per se – these were all adults), I've been obsessed with the idea of putting together systems in which pussy would be delivered to you through little or no effort of your own – essentially, using "lifestyle design" to pull an end run on natural selection.

Call it The 4-Hour Sex Life.

The classic example would be the Hollywood producer who bangs a lot of chicks on his casting couch. A guy like that wouldn't even have to bathe on a regular basis, if he didn't want to, and he'd still be able to score. He'd be living the dream. In fact, there's a few guys in pron who look gross and are said to not smell right, and yet obviously they're cleaning up. Well, figuratively speaking. Video evidence of this is available on the Internets, I've been told.

Wildly manipulative and wrong though it may be (I'm officially against it, sincerely), it's probably not against the law, as long as there's no definite quid pro quo. Kanye West has at least dabbled in this kind of behavior. He cast Amber Rose in one of his videos and then dated her for a period of time. If him putting a finger on that wasn't a condition of her employment, it was at least facilitated by her being there on the set. That's what I mean by lifestyle design.

By the way, before we get into any unsavory subject matter, I should warn you that this is not some bowdlerized, Tiger Beat-style account of Kanye's life and career. Kanye West is married to a woman who sells DVDs of herself being split in two by Brandy's little brother. For a living. The most recent Kanye West album, as I'm writing this, has songs about eating an Asian girl's pussy with duck sauce, and shoving his fist in a black girl's pussy "like a civil rights sign." If you're the kind of person who requires a book that somehow discusses these things without mentioning them, you've picked up the wrong book. You accidentally wandered away from the section of the bookstore that has toys in it, where you belong.

That man-ho blood coursing through his veins led a young Kanye to develop what ended up becoming a lifelong interest in pornography. It's been one of the few constants in his life, along with music and tiny jackets. Even his beloved mother is no longer with us arguably due in part to Kanye's fascination with pron.

Kanye's mom, whom he lived with more often than not, kept a collection of 1980s Ron Jeremy-style VHS pron. Which seems weird to me. I know, because PronHub keeps detailed statistics about who visits their site (ruh roh), that some girls watch pron. But how many women had a pron collection on VHS? I think most people just rented pron back during the VHS era. To actually buy those tapes cost an arm and a leg – it required a certain level of commitment to pronography. So Kanye's father wasn't the only one with, erm, proclivities. That may have even been how they found each other.

Donda West first discovered her son's fascination with pron when he snuck and watched one of her VHS tapes and accidentally left it in the VCR for her to find. Awkward! The easiest thing to do in a situation like that is just put the tape back where it belongs and let the situation blow over without either of you mentioning it. Imagine how difficult it would be to have a conversation with an eight year-old kid about pron, let alone your own pron, the shit that you specifically picked out at an off brand video store in a sketchy strip mall, because it best-suited your "needs." I shudder to think what kind of pron this was.

What does an eight year-old boy even do with pron? As a 33 year-old man, I've got videos I've been watching since I was like 26 that I haven't seen any more than about eight minutes of, because… well, there's no need to get too graphic here. Kids might want to read this book. I'm hoping my elementary school alma mater will keep it in their library. When I was a kid, back in the mid to late '80s, they had that book where the guy who played Carlton on the Fresh Prince of Bel Air teaches you how to break dance, and I think putting this book alongside it would provide me with a certain not necessarily pron-related sense of completion – an emotional money shot, if you will.

A young Kanye probably sat there and watched those videos all the way through, while his mom was off working on her dissertation. Pron films are always especially long, to justify charging so much for them. There's one scene with the chick who's on the cover, and then they pad the length with a few chicks who aren't attractive enough to carry their own film. In fact, Kanye may have forgotten to put the tape back where he found it because he sat there so long he ended up falling asleep and having a dream about Christy Canyon.

This is all speculation, mind you.

There was also an incident in which Kanye brought some nudie magazines to class and got caught passing them around to other kids so everyone could get a good look. How considerate of him. In retrospect, this was a precursor to his career casting a lot of skanky chicks with ginormous cans in videos like Drake's "Best I Ever Had," let alone any number of his own videos.

The teacher asked Kanye where he got those magazines, and he said his mother's closet, which, again... worrisome. Kanye's mom was called to the school, where she slapped him and then took him home and forced him to write a paper about why kids shouldn't look at pron. This was all discussed in the book Donda wrote about raising Kanye. I didn't read it back when it came out, and the budget I had to write this book wasn't sufficient to buy a copy (the library didn't have it), but I remember reading an article about it in the Daily Mail or somewhere back when it came out. I may have written about it – or at least mentioned it – back when I was with XXL.

Anyway, Freud would have had a field day with that one: The fact that Kanye's mom wrote an entire book about raising him. The fact that she had all of that pron. The fact that she slapped him, which may have later resulted in masochistic tendencies. And the fact that she made him write a research paper about his precocious interest in pron, thus forever linking education, punishment, pronography and his mother in his not yet fully formed, already depraved mind. Oh, what I wouldn't give to get my hands on a copy of that paper. Is it typed in ALL CAPS?

Before her body completely fell apart, Kanye's mom would sometimes bring home men to have sex with. Whether these were men she would meet at bars or students (or perhaps even maintenance staff) from the university I'm not sure – it doesn't say in the song "Mama's Boyfriend."

In that song, Kanye talks about hearing sex sounds coming from his mom's bedroom and fantasizing about wanting to kill those guys, and I'm pretty sure he didn't mean it in an I'm-deeply-upset-with-this-person sort of way, but rather in a my-mind-honestly-just-went-to-committing-murder sort of way.

If I were Kim Kardashian, I'd be concerned about sleeping in the same room as Kanye (if they really do share a bed), let alone having him around their child. It's already been proven that those Kardashians can't tell a decent black man from a crackhead. They see that dark complexion and their mind just goes to vigorous lovemaking. You know the mother fucked OJ, right? #allegedly

If there really was a football player named D'Vigorous Lover, he'd almost certainly be dating a Kardashian.

Chastened, inappropriately sexualized and lacking a proper male influence, Kanye developed an interest in visual art and writing poetry. Ayo.

It says in the world's most accurate encyclopedia that when he was 13 he wrote a song called "Green Eggs and Ham." I've never heard the song itself, but the title is ripped off from Dr. Seuss. The lyrics may have been as well – it's just not possible to say. As was the case with the nudie magazines in class, this was a precursor to his music career, in which he won a Grammy for a song he didn't write and later was widely rumored to employ a team of ghost producers, in addition to the group of kids who write his rhymes, thus having very little creative input into his own music. Ironically, many of the rhymes he obviously did write are Dr. Seuss-like in their simplicity, though not involving delicious breakfast meats.

If Kanye's mom was aware that "Green Eggs and Ham" was really just the book by Dr. Seuss in rap form – if, perhaps, that was something she taught in the English department at Chicago State University – she didn't discourage Kanye from passing it off as his own work. Instead she let him talk her into paying $25 an hour for studio time to make a recording, with a setup that didn't consist of anything other than a microphone dangling from the ceiling, suspended by a bent coat hanger, in some guy's dingy basement. It's a wonder nothing sexual happened down there – as far as I know.

If Kanye's father had been in the picture, he could have at least talked ("jewed") the price down to $20 an hour. Women don't have the sense to negotiate in situations like that. That's why car salesmen love to see a woman coming. A man, confronted with a ridiculous price, will just be like, "Fuck you," and walk out. "Call me at the end of the month when you dumbasses haven't met your quota and your family's on the verge of getting kicked out on the street." But really, I don't see why he couldn't have just dangled a microphone from the ceiling in his own basement and plugged it into a tape recorder. If Kanye used more than an hour of studio time, he already paid for the price of that microphone. You can get a microphone from Office Max for like $9. Hence podcasting. It might not be the same thing Michael Jackson used to record Thriller, but neither was the shit in that guy's basement.

Now an important member of the Chicago hip-hop community, young Kanye was introduced to No ID, the guy who produced the first two Common albums. No ID taught Kanye how to use a sampler, and the rest – as they say – is history. As is said in a courtroom, Kanye took to sampling like a duck to water. Philosophically, it was not unlike the process he used to "write" the lyrics to "Green Eggs and Ham": you're not coming up with music on your own, you're taking music someone else already came up with and slightly re-arranging it.

Which is not to say that using a sampler is an invalid way of making rap music, mind you. On the contrary, using a sampler is the only valid way of making rap music. Attempting to make your own music, using musical instruments, is unacceptable. You just end up sounding like The Roots. To his credit, Kanye, when he was actually producing his own records, was a great producer. Credit where credit is due. Though even then his talent was largely squandered producing for people I didn't need to hear rap, above all himself and a post-2000 Jay-Z.

Kanye graduated from a high school in an affluent suburb and received a scholarship to paint at an art school in Chicago. He was well on his way to becoming one of those guys who just pay some poor kid slave wages to paint their pictures for them, which they then sell to a hedge fund manager for like $10 million. The hedge fund managers could give a rat's ass who really painted it, in part because that's like two and a half hours pay for them and in part because they wouldn't know from good art anyway, nor would anyone who visits their ridonkulously large houses. They're just buying it for the brand name. That's how the art industry works. There was an article in GQ a while back about this guy Kehinde Wiley. All he does is go over to Africa and snap photos of poor kids with flies on their faces, and then he's got – quite literally – a room full of people over in China who paint his pictures for him.

At a family reunion once – these were my father's relatives, and I think this was here in St. Louis – this fat lady whom my uncle was married to at the time stood up to give a sort of testimony. This was part of the event. She spoke of how blessed she was to have finally found a man who was willing to, among other things, "lay hands" on her when necessary, thus confirming a suspicion I've long had about at least some women. She talked about her work as a painter, and one of the things she said was that you have to be careful who you show your paintings to, because they'll have "a room full of Chinamen" making unauthorized reproductions of your work. That's the source of the phrase I sometimes use when a conversation turns to bootlegging.

The more you know...

I'm surprised Kanye never got into this racket. He's been involved in various other creative pursuits besides just looping up old R&B songs on a laptop computer, including his many failed attempts at starting his own clothing line. He could potentially make even more money as a visual artist than as a rapper – and using similar "techniques." He's already got the name recognition, which is the key to being able to demand a premium. I know he once showed off a few paintings he did in high school, on the same MTV special in which he took a bold stance against homophobia, but the purpose there may have been to make a statement about not acquiescing to traditional notions of masculinity.

Kanye was only in art school for a hot minute before he transferred to Chicago State, where his mom worked, to study English. His mom was the head of the English department.

If this was because he wasn't a very good painter, then that was a shortsighted decision, and I bet he now regrets it. Whatever, if anything, he could have picked up in art college could have aided him in a career as a celebrity painter (in the same way that Paris Hilton is a celebrity DJ), rather than trying to pursue a sideline as an ostensibly straight male fashion designer.

His grades couldn't have been that bad, because what do they even test you on in art college? Was he holding his brush at the wrong angle? Nullus. Since the value of art is subjective in nature, he could argue that anything he painted that wasn't very good was really a modern art masterpiece. He was only there for maybe a year, if that, and I happen to know that you can't lose a college scholarship in less than a year. They give you that first semester for free – if you don't spend it getting drunk every night of the week and sleeping all day the next day, you're basically just throwing away money. If you fuck up second semester, they just put you on probation. Which means that you could not so much as crack open a book and spend three semesters in college for free. You could go three semesters without even buying a book. I went to college on a full scholarship (must have been some sort of clerical error) and managed to hold on to it for a good three years just by calling down to the administrative building and explaining that I realize that I fucked up and next semester I'm gonna try much harder; this time I really mean it.

Similarly, Kanye was in a position in which he could have studied at Chicago State indefinitely without having to convince anyone that he was somehow an asset to the university. Not only did his mom work there, she was head of the English department. Some schools let you attend for free if your parent is just a janitor or some shit. (They probably get some sort of tax break for doing so.) Shit, if my mom was a college professor, I'd still be in college today. It'd be worth it just to sit in rooms full of 19 year-old girls. I miss that smell. It'd almost be worth listening to some dumbass who couldn't hack it in the real world stand there and pontificate. It wouldn't matter whether or not I paid attention and thus if I did very well on the exams. I've already got a degree. I'm just there for what you might call cultural enrichment. It's not like I've got shit else better to do during the afternoons. And if I had like seven degrees, someone would have to finally offer me a job that pays more than $10 an hour, wouldn't they? That should be a law.

Instead Kanye decided he wanted to be a record producer. He couldn't handle both the course load at Chicago State University and looping up old '70s-era R&B records on a sampler and adjusting the pitch setting. This ought to come as a surprise to anyone who's ever actually been to college. A college semester is only something like 16 weeks – of a year that consists of 52 weeks. And of those 16 weeks, you're only spending a few hours in class. Maybe three or four hours a day, tops. Some days of the week, I only spent like 50 minutes in class. Even if you spend four hours a day in class, every day of the week, that still leaves, like, a shedload of time to watch Wonder Years and Family Ties reruns on ABC Family, play Soul Calibur on Sega Dreamcast, walk down to the gas station on the corner and cop a tall boy of Miller Genuine Draft, fap to Internets pron and take a nap. At least, that's how I imagine someone might spend an afternoon in college. I should have seriously considered becoming a record producer.

Kanye quickly became a ghost producer for Derek "D-Dot" Angelettie, who did a lot of work on the second (and final) Biggie Smalls album, Life After Death. He was the guy who did those Madd Rapper skits. Yo son, tell 'em why you mad! This was a formative period for Kanye, in that it established a couple of different patterns in his career. First of all, if you don't count Chicago hip-hop, which doesn't matter to me personally, this was the beginning of Kanye squandering his talent producing songs for people I don't need to hear rap. He had beats on the second Foxy Brown album, the Harlem World album and the Madd Rapper album, which really is a thing that exists. Second, working with D-Dot may have normalized for Kanye the idea of taking someone else's work and passing it off as your own, as the work he did during that period was mostly credited to D-Dot. He was already at least somewhat familiar with the process from his earliest days as a "lyricist" and from having attended art school, however briefly. Later he would be rumored to employ a staff of ghost producers, in addition to the kids who write his lyrics, raising the question of to what extent, if any, Kanye contributes to his own albums. If I had the means, I might pay a group of people to put together an album for me.

Jay-Z paid Kanye to make a few beats for the long-since-forgotten Dynasty album, which I remember kinda liking at the time. I think it began life as a Rocafella Records compilation and then Jay-Z – or probably someone at Def Jam – realized they could make way more money calling it a Jay-Z album, so there's way more weed carrier verses on it than you require – with everyone on that album whose name isn't Jay-Z being a weed carrier, for the purpose of this discussion. Kanye would go on to be Jay-Z's main collaborator on his next album, the overrated Blueprint, and many of the albums he's released subsequently. This proved to be a fortuitous pairing for both of them, in that Jay-Z was one of the few rappers left at that point with the kind of budget to afford Kanye's wanton sampling, and Kanye helped keep Jay-Z relevant for a few years after he ran out of good ideas, until his own career settled into a sort of self-sustaining state of tabloid celebrity. As is said of relationships between people who met at a special meeting after Sunday School, they were good for each other.

But what Kanye really wanted to do was rap. Jay-Z, who owned a rap label that would sign seemingly anyone, wouldn't pay him any mind, because at the end of the day Jay-Z is still an MC. He's the guy who once recorded Reasonable Doubt. Kanye doesn't just spit simple Cat in the Hat rhymes like the RZA complained about on the intro to disc two of Wu-Tang Forever, the Realest Words That Will Ever Be Spoken, he really did rhyme cat with hat. Damon Dash finally signed Kanye as a rapper just so he'd continue making beats for Jay-Z albums. I guess he figured, they let Memphis Bleek release albums. How bad can it be? They found a shampoo commercial for Memphis Bleek, and he doesn't even have any hair.

I thought The College Dropout was terrible, but apparently I was in the minority. It went on to be one of the most critically acclaimed albums of its era, for what it's worth, topping the Village Voice's Pazz and Jop critics poll and winning multiple Grammys, including Best Rap Song for "Jesus Walks." It remains his best-selling album, to this day. I'd liked some of the shit Kanye produced on the past few Jay-Z albums and some of the work he'd done for various other artists, but The College Dropout to me was the sound of Kanye indulging a lot of his worst instincts. Employing gospel choirs, violin players, people singing through vocoders and what have you, Kanye was trying too hard to convince people that he was a genius. As if. His ego got the best of him. In that album I could see everything that would eventually go wrong with his career.

Kanye quickly followed up The College Dropout with '05's Late Registration, one of the few other Kanye albums I've heard. Eschewing the sped up soul sample sound he pioneered with the Blueprint, which had been played out a good two years before College Dropout came out, I found it to be more listenable than its predecessor. It didn't sell quite as many copies, but the song "Gold Digger" might still be his biggest hit single to date. It's arguably the best thing Kanye ever did. I only hesitate to say for certain because I think it should be left up to someone with more of an interest in the matter to make that designation.

"Gold Digger," in retrospect, may have been intended in part as a message to the girl he was engaged to at the time, Alexis Phifer. Though not half bad-looking, she was no Kim Kardashian, in the sense that she wasn't making $50 million a year just to go outside once a day in a questionably appropriate outfit and have her picture taken. An aspiring fashion designer, her line probably didn't make it any further than Kanye's own line, which is to say that it went quite literally nowhere. Kanye wasn't about to marry her, have her divorce him just because he was constantly standing on tables and declaring himself a genius, and end up on the front page of the National Enquirer looking like Johnny Carson after he lost Half.

I don't think he was really interested in marrying her anyway. Since he dropped her like a bad habit, he's been in two major relationships and he's been pictured in night clubs and what have you with any number of random skanks, all of whom were either white or... you know, white-ish. White enough to qualify for a contract on an iPhone without bringing the deed to her mother's house down to the Apple store as collateral. Girls with dat privilege. Like many a black man who hasn't already permanently disappointed his mother (I would imagine), Kanye may have felt pressure to marry a black chick. He didn't want to suffer the indignity of hearing his mom mutter snide remarks about his white wife under her breath on Thanksgiving, or maybe even prepare a separate set of dishes with no seasoning (just the way they like it) for the special guest – separate but not equal. I imagine these are things that go on in interracial families at Thanksgiving.

Kanye's mom died in a tragic plastic surgery mishap, thus freeing him to act a damn fool, to the extent that he wasn't already. She was getting both liposuction and breast implants, at the ripe old age of like 60. This was a few years still before the onslaught of VH-1 hoodrat reality series – at that point there may have just been that show with Flavor Flav and Sylvester Stallone's improbably bonerific ex-trophy wife from back during the Rocky IV era – so I'm at a loss for why she even needed all this surgery. She must have been making a pretty good living as Kanye's manager, charging 15% of whatever he was making, i.e. probably like millions. I'm sure she could have found a guy to take advantage of her, regardless of what her tits looked like. I think I speak for most black guys when I say that money is the one thing I actually don't need from a woman. As long as it doesn't bother her that I'm not contributing anything at all to the relationship financially, I could care less how much money she has.

She could have all the money in the world or no money at all. I can't fuck a pile of money. (Well, I could.) I already live in the ghetto, so for me dating a broke chick is just a shorter drive.

Kanye's mom may have internalized the western standard of beauty as presented in so many Kanye West music videos. He cast Anna Nicole Smith in the video for "The New Workout Plan" and Pam Anderson in the video for "Touch the Sky." Those were the two most lusted after pairs of cans of the 1990s, when Kanye and I were both in high school. They both may have been in some of those issues of Playboy Kanye found in his mom's closet. They were definitely in Playboy. I think Pam Anderson was on the cover of at least two Playboys I bought after I was old enough to start buying Playboy, i.e. a kinda old-looking (at least to white people) 16. I only just now remembered, as I was typing (ahem, writing) this, how many Playboys and various other nudie magazines I bought back in the day. What a waste. Day in and day out I see chicks on Instagram and what have you way hotter than maybe anyone who was in Playboy the entire decade of the 1990s – admittedly, not their peak. If Anna Nicole Smith were born in, say, 1993, she never would have advanced beyond manning the flour table at a fried chicken restaurant. I wouldn't trust her on register. She didn't seem to have the intellect.

In a sense, Kanye killed his own mother. She did what she could to try to curtail his youthful fascination with pronography, forcing him to write that essay, which in retrospect may have doomed him to drop out of school, but there was nothing she could do to stop Kanye from doing what he wanted to do. If she hid it in her closet, he'd just find it and take it to school. The same indomitable spirit that would later lead him to drop out of two different schools he was going to for free, pursue a career as a rapper despite the fact that he can't rap, record his first single with his jaw wired shut, so on and so forth, led him to defy his mother, and his mind was warped at an early age as a result. He suffered from delusions of grandeur because he knew that he couldn't make enough money to make sweet, passionate love to the kind of girls he saw in Playboy as, say, a lowly English professor, and it was that desire to miscegenate that fueled his rise to the very top of the music industry – what seemed like the result extreme self-confidence was really just sex addiction manifesting itself as creative energy as a means to an end, with that end being his life becoming a pron film of sorts: He would cast girls he saw in Playboy in his videos. He would marry a girl who first became famous for making a sex tape with Ray J. Together they would reenact scenes from Kim K Superstar, ultimately resulting in the birth of a daughter he'd name North West, possibly as a tribute to Peter North, who blew some of the biggest loads of all time, of ALL TIME. Kanye West once produced a song called "Two Words," Peter North was known for shooting three ropes. CONNECT THE DOTS PEOPLE. Kanye may have pursued Kim Kardashian in part because frequent Peter North co-star Christy Canyon is Armenian. This shit is deep.

On a certain level, I feel like I've only scratched the surface. While my knowledge of modern pron is legendary in corners of the Internets you don't even want to know about, I only know but so much about the old stuff. My mom didn't keep a secret cache of magazines and videos that I could regularly access. Nor did my old man, who lived there as well. Who'd a thunkit?

2
You Didn't Build That

Kanye West and I are alike in that we place no value on education. We differ in that I have an education and he doesn't.

Granted, I'm only educated in the most nominal sense of the term, meaning that I stayed in school all the way up through college and then I received a diploma. I didn't get kicked out for fighting and end up either having to spend a semester at Hope High School, or falling victim to what's known amongst progressives as the School to Prison Pipeline. Because I'm a guy, there's no way I could have gotten pregnant and had to drop out to take care of my kid, though I certainly would have enjoyed the process. (If I'd managed to get a girl pregnant, obviously I wouldn't have dropped out of school.) Like Kanye, it didn't cost me shit to go to college. I was there on scholarship. When the school eventually thought better of that idea, my parents were able to scrape together and cut a check.

At the end of four years, I had more or less enough credits to graduate, but my grades were only good enough to graduate with the college equivalent of a GED – a general studies degree, or something to that effect. Essentially, the business department, which was my major, didn't want to put their stamp on someone who spent four years sitting around playing Sega Dreamcast, listening to MF Doom and checking ABC Family to see if they were airing the Soleil Moon Frye episode of the Wonder Years. (They played that particular episode once every few weeks, for the benefit of a certain kind of individual.) You had to have a B+ average just to get a degree, which was silly, because if literally everyone who ever went there got good grades then what difference does it make? I had to take a whole fifth year and more or less ace it, to boost my average. I was fortunate in that I was just barely capable intellectually.

A kindly white woman taught me how to read, like in the movie Dangerous Minds, and that helped.

It ended up being all for naught. I graduated, and I was barely able to get a job in fast food, let alone a quote-unquote real job. And you know how a fruitless job search can be bad for your mental health. I spent a couple of years getting turned down for all kinds of jobs. One time I came close to getting a job signing black people up for subprime loans, but there was some concern that my blaccent wasn't strong enough. Black people won't buy exploitative financial products from just anyone. They need to feel it's someone they can trust. The help I received in college, sounding out my words and learning how to conjugate the verb "to be" actually kinda fucked me in the ass. It was the educational equivalent of a smallpox blanket. Sometimes white people think they're doing you a favor but they're not. Eventually, I settled into a life of what you might call Subsistence Content Farming, which more or less continues to this day.

Kanye figured prominently into my career as a blogger, to the point where when I made it to the front page of the local fish wrap here in the STL, it was mostly due to a campaign I led to have him banned from the Grammys. A lot of my relatives, who don't all use the Intenets, saw that issue, and they remain under the impression that I antagonize Kanye West via the Internets for a living, which is an actual job you can get, when in reality I antagonize all kinds of people and I also collect pictures of certain kinds of women. I wish all I had to do was antagonize Kanye West! And it's not much of a living either, I should point out.

Initially, I was kinda indifferent towards Kanye West. I liked the beats he did on albums like The Blueprint well enough. The Blueprint dropped when I was a junior in college, the same day as the Twin Towers, though only the illiterate hadn't already had it for like two weeks at that point. This is something to keep in mind when people on the Internets cite the fact that it was released on 9/11 as part of the reason it's a classic.

I didn't think Kanye West was a very good rapper, but then there's a lot of people who I don't think are very good rappers. Especially in 2004. I never became so inextricably linked to, say, "Lean Back"-era Fat Joe, aside from sharing a similar physique. I reviewed The College Dropout for my blog in the spring of 2004. I was nearing the end of my "victory lap," at the time, maybe two months shy of graduation. I'd already been blogging for a few years, but I'd recently redoubled my efforts. I had to give up my afternoon cans of Miller Genuine Draft, lest I end up in college indefinitely. I was experiencing a lot of anxiety with regard to my grades, which would continue for years.

Into my 30s now, I still have that dream where I just realized there's a class I signed up for that I haven't been to all semester. I read recently that ecstasy cures PTSD. I'm thinking about trying it out, but I figure as long as I'm gonna ingest something that chews holes in your brain like Swiss cheese, I might as well do it at an EDM festival full of girls I can touch inappropriately, to to get the full effect – which might even be necessary to cure PTSD. The thing is, I'm not sure what EDM is, but I can't imagine I would enjoy it. I might put an ad up on Craigslist and see what happens. If any girls reading this want to do drugs in my basement and get "tampered with" to the sweet sounds of the King Gheedorah album, email me. No law enforcement, pls.

I figured I might like the production on The College Dropout and not really care for the rhymes, but come to find out I didn't really care for any of it. The problem with the rappin' was to be expected. My ears have been ruined from years spent sitting around listening to people who actually know what they're doing – I can't just listen to anything. I didn't choose the boom bap dinosaur life, the boom bap dinosaur life chose me. If the beat was intended to be the primary focus, it would be called beat music, not rap music. Not only will I listen to an album with great lyrics and "boring" production, I'll sit around and listen to that album all day long. I've got the time.

Surprisingly, I found the production on The College Dropout to be much more obnoxious than anything I'd heard from Kanye up until that point. He added a lot of elements to the mix that ended up having the opposite of their intended effect: They didn't strike me as genius. As a hip-hop head, I'm not impressed by production techniques that involve anything other than coming up with slight variations on the exact same drum sounds over and over and over again. It seemed to me that Kanye was more concerned with being viewed as brilliant than making music I had any use for personally, like his ego may have been getting the best of him. Little did I know.

Maybe a week before I graduated from college I called White Castle, where I worked during the summer and while I was on break, to let them know when I'd be back in town. I was ready to begin what I'd later jokingly refer to as my post-graduate work. I did in fact earn a certificate in food safety from ServSafe. Last year I found it in a box in my garage, looking for my copy of Wu-Tang Forever. I posted a picture of it on Instagram. People seemed to enjoy that. They may not have believed it when I wrote about it in my first book The Mindset of a Champion. Ironically, I have no idea where my college diploma is. The manager at White Castle actually called me the day of graduation and asked me if I could work the night shift that evening. I thought it over for a second, and then I figured what the fuck. I was gonna have to settle into my career as a fast food wage slave at some point. Why not the same day the president of the university handed me my diploma?

That afternoon, before I got back to St. Louis, my parents took me to a Red Lobster in Columbia, MO, the same city where I got laughed at by those girls. It's only right that black achievement is celebrated with Crab Meats. That was the one time in my life I had those lobster nachos. Of course they were delicious. But later I read that the "lobster bites" you get at a Long John Silver aren't really lobster, they're hermit crab, and I've come to suspect that's also the case with the lobster nachos at Red Lobster.

At White Castle, I settled into an unfortunate pattern that involved gorging myself on the free meals they gave you, probably because they received some sort of tax break similar to what grocery stores get for hiring retarded kids. I wrote about it extensively in Mindset. I was making like $600 a month, and I was paying about $233 (i.e. one-third of $800) in rent: I couldn't afford to buy food.

I had these boxes of Rolling Stone magazines that had accumulated at my parents' house while I was in college. Initially, I left them sitting there when I moved out, maybe 10 days after I graduated, in part to avoid having to listen to my parents hassle me about my inability to find a quote-unquote real job. This became a bit of an issue. I didn't want to take the magazines with me, because there was only but so much space in the place where I was living, but I didn't want to throw them out either, because I figured I might want to read them one day.

Eventually I was issued an ultimatum: Either I had to take them with me, or they were going out by the curb. They may have even been set out by the curb, and I had to go retrieve them – I can't remember anymore. At any rate, I started to go through them and pick out the issues I might like to read. There were at least as many issues of VIBE as Rolling Stone. The first issue of VIBE I picked up had Brandy or someone on the cover, and it occurred to me: Why do I need a single issue of VIBE? I had what you might call a Peter Gibbons Moment. I separated the magazines into piles and set the VIBE out by the curb.

One day on my lunch break I read an article on Kanye in Rolling Stone. This was from around the time when The College Dropout was released, so it may have only been a few months old at that point. In this article, they spoke with Kanye's mother, who would end up ditching her job at Chicago State to become his manager – though I'm not sure if she was really managing him or if he was just cutting her a check for 15%. Is it necessary for a manager to know anything at all about rap music or how the music biz works?

Kanye's mother spoke of how much of a genius he is, how she spoiled him as a child, and how she tried to instill in him his ridonkulous sense of self-confidence. She just couldn't get over how brilliant it was that he uses the term safe belt in "Through the Wire," she said, because safety belt doesn't quite fit with the rhyme scheme. Who else would have thought to do that? She seemed to be more impressed with Kanye than anyone other than Kanye himself. Meanwhile, I don't know that I've ever heard anyone use the term safety belt to refer to a seat belt.

It was at that point that I realized that whatever was wrong with Kanye must have had to do with his mother. That afternoon I went home and wrote a post called "Let's hunt and kill Kanye West's mother." The title of course was a reference to the bit on Bill Hicks' masterful Rant in E Minor about a show he pitched to ABC called Let's Hunt and Kill Billy Ray Cyrus. ABC execs were on the fence about the show, he said, until he assured them that there would be titty. At that point he became a producer. He never knew it was so easy.

I wasn't actually suggesting we chase Kanye's mom through the woods with a shotgun like a big, black cock of death, mind you. Not that it matters at this point. But I feel like I should point that out because later there was an issue with a similar post I wrote about Kanye's Eskimo brother Ray J, which of course will be discussed elsewhere here, in the chapter on the film Ray J made with Kanye's baby's mother. I was just pointing out that Kanye's mom seemed to be the source of a lot of what was wrong with him.

Regardless, I was inundated with comments and email from people upset about the post, including people claiming to be various relatives, his childhood babysitter, and even Kanye's mom herself. She said she'd come home from one of Kanye's shows, Googled herself and was surprised to see that someone was advocating chasing her through the wood with a shotgun. I guess that would be surprising. It makes you wonder how often Kanye and his mom (before she died getting her cans fixed) Google themselves.

Some of those people rushing to Kanye's defense were probably bummy relatives hoping Kanye would see that they'd been on the Internets issuing death threats on his behalf and cut them a check. They knew he'd Google himself, because they've known him since he was a child. Why else would someone think to go on the Internets to defend their relatives from trolls in comments sections? I don't have any relatives who are famous, but I do have relatives who are likely to turn up in the news. Anything that's said about them in a comments section is probably true anyway.

It was pointed out to me by some young guy in the comments section of my blog that Kanye didn't really write the lyrics to "Jesus Walks." Kanye's various relatives, his childhood babysitter and his mom had no way of responding to this, because this could easily be verified by downloading the Rhymefest version of the song from one of those illegal file transfer sites that probably installed dangerous software on your computer. This was a while still before you could easily pull up the audio to almost anything on YouTube. But I noticed, when I checked just now, that you can't find the original "Jesus Walks" on YouTube. Kanye must have personally had it scrubbed from the Internets.

There's a couple of videos labeled the original "Jesus Walks," or Rhymefest's verse from "Jesus Walks," but they're really just some freestyle Rhymefest once spit in which he mentions the fact that he wrote one of the verses from "Jesus Walks." The real Rhymefest version of "Jesus Walks" is a much more damning piece of audio. Listening to it, you can hear where Kanye uses the exact same words, the same delivery and everything. Essentially, the Rhymefest version functioned as a reference track for the Kanye version, not unlike the audio you can dig up of Biggie Smalls doing the lyrics he wrote for Lil Kim songs like "Queen Bitch," complete with references to guys eating his pussy.

The only difference between the Kanye version and the Rhymefest version of "Jesus Walks" is that Kanye inserts his own name in places where Rhymefest had said his name in the original. He was lucky Kanye West rhymes with Rhymefest. Jesus really was looking out for him. Otherwise, I'm not sure what he would have done. He may have had to change his name to something that rhymes with Rhymefest. Lime Vest perhaps. His mom would have hailed him as a genius for doing so.

Maybe a week before I found out that Kanye West didn't really write "Jesus Walks" the nominations for that year's Grammys were announced. Kanye had been nominated for several awards – seemingly more than should have been possible for a rap artist, given that there's only a few rap categories. "Jesus Walks" was nominated for Best Rap Song. I didn't think it was a very good song anyway, and once I found out about the fraud behind its creation it seemed ridiculous to me that it could potentially win an award. This was about to be Milli Vanilli receiving an award for a song they didn't sing all over again, except that Kanye probably wouldn't be forced to hold a press conference in which he gave the award back a few weeks later.

MFN Puff Daddy won a Grammy back in 1998, and all it resulted in was Ol' Dirty Bastard rushing the stage as Shawn Colvin was accepting an award for "Sunny Came Home" and declaring that while Puffy was good, Wu-Tang is the best; Wu-Tang is for the children. The Recording Academy doesn't hold black music in general to the same standards as white music, and they don't hold rap music to much of a standard period. That's why they don't show the rap awards on TV: they have no idea who they might be giving those statues to. I'm convinced they don't even listen to the music. They couldn't look at Milli Vanilli and know that what they were really hearing was the sound of two old Civil Rights-era black guys and a woman – three people total. As a social experiment, I might show up one year and accept an award on behalf of Rick Ross.

So I came up with a plan: I would circulate a petition in which I explain that Kanye West shouldn't be allowed to win an award because he didn't really write his own rhymes, and it would be ridiculous to give a Grammy to a rapper who didn't write his own rhymes. In rap music it's understood that the guy standing on stage saying rhymes wrote those rhymes himself. If he didn't, he's trying to pull a fast one on you. Technically, he might be guilty of fraud. I'd have to consult with a lawyer. Unless it's someone like the DOC, who can't talk anymore, due to drunk driving, there's no reason why the guy who wrote the song can't just perform it himself. Rap music isn't sophisticated enough that the quality of the guy's voice matters. If an artist's voice is especially obnoxious, it might be hailed as "more interesting" than regular rap music by the New Yorker. He could be the next Timbaland.

If Rhymefest had recorded "Jesus Walks" himself, it wouldn't have been nearly as popular, in part because Rhymefest looks like a big, black, ugly gorilla, and he's not talented enough to where that would be a non-issue, like Biggie Smalls. There was a similar situation back in the early '90s, when C+C Music Factory would perform that song "Everybody Dance Now" with a hot chick dancing around on stage like she was the one singing. Meanwhile, there was some fat chick standing behind a curtain doing all of the heavy lifting. Really, you should have been able to tell from listening to the song that the hot chick wasn't the one singing. They were similar to Milli Vanilli, in that sense. The Grammys, in giving awards to rappers who don't even write their own lyrics, promote this kind of discrimination.

It seems like there used to be a lot more of those sites where you can start your own petition. People probably stopped bothering with them once they realized they didn't do any good. There was a new petition circling the Internets every day back in the mid '00s, and I doubt very many, if any, of them achieved their stated goal. Usually, I wouldn't even bother reading them. If it was something I really needed to know, they could have just told me. I wouldn't appreciate someone circulating a petition having to do with me personally, because I wouldn't want that many people knowing that some aspect of my life is problematic.

The one time I can recall a petition even seeming like it might have worked was when Pat Buchanan was fired from MSNBC for writing a book about how America is running out of white people. (Who will discriminate against black people?) And even in that case it seemed more like a group realizing he was already on his way out the door and trying to take credit for it. The same group couldn't get anyone fired from XXL back when the rap magazine ran a video in which Too Short gave middle school-age kids advice about non-consensual fingerbanging. And XXL lives to fire people!

This was a while still before there was such a thing as Facebook. If that site was around at all, it was still just something Mark Zuckerberg put together to harvest personal information about the girls at Harvard rather than trying to strike up a conversation with any of them. MySpace was probably around, but MySpace was never really good for anything other than becoming "friends" with emo bands. After everyone stopped using it, prostitutes started using it to sell pussy. That probably continued until they remodeled it and started running a lot of music articles. Now it's completely useless.

My only hope for spreading the petition was to (a) post it on my own blog, and (b) try to get anyone else I knew with a blog to post it on their blog. Most people's blogs were only ever read by one or two people and maybe the occasional stalker, so in effect I was just posting it on my own blog. I could have emailed it to people, but the only email addresses I had were the bum rappers and their representatives who spammed my inbox day in and day out, and they probably would have gotten pissed if I turned around and did the exact same thing to them. I don't have any friends (natch), and I haven't been as proactive about harvesting the email addresses of people who visit my blog as I should be.

In order to spread the word about the petition, I sent out a press release using one of those sites you can use to send out a free press release. I had read, back when I was in college, that a lot of the news your read in the paper is really just press releases reprinted more or less verbatim. And I saw some video in college, in one of my marketing classes, about how some of the segments on local TV news broadcasts are put together by marketing companies. These free press release sites brag about the number of media organizations they deliver press releases to. They claim to deliver press releases to seemingly every media organization there ever was. I figured, if I wrote one that seemed professional enough, maybe a few of them would pick it up and run it as actual news.

Part of the registration process for the site involved entering your phone number. I put my actual phone number and didn't think anything of it. You upload a press release to this site a while before it's set to be sent out, in part so it can be approved. Maybe the next afternoon, I got a call from a guy from the press release site. He said for like $25 there was some advanced distribution I could sign up for. Essentially, it was conveyed to me that for free all they did was send it to an email list that was probably forwarded to a spam folder wherever it was received. For $25 they'd send it to people's actual email addresses. Supposedly.

I figured it was only $25, and I just happened to have $25 to my name at that particular moment, and this was easily the best thing I ever did on my blog and maybe the only important thing I'll ever do in my life. Why not just spend the $25? I gave the guy my credit card information over the phone. The good news is that all they did with it was charge me $25 that one time. I didn't unwittingly end up signing up for a lifetime subscription to Chinese dietary supplements that's impossible to unsubscribe to. The bad news is that advanced distribution is the public relations equivalent of the "transmission flush" at Jiffy Lube: it's just a surcharge for the terminally gullible. You don't actually get anything for it.

My press release was never ever picked up by NBC or anyone as a result of uploading it to that service, but what I did was, I just sent it out manually to a few rap music blogs and websites, and some of them picked up on it. A few sites passed on it and then ended up running it anyway after they saw that other sites were running it. I guess they didn't want their competition to have the "exclusive," regardless of what it was. The hip-hop blogosphere is the worst.

One of the top black morning radio shows – I think it was Tom Joyner, but don't start me to lying – mentioned it during their news segment. Apparently that's how they get their news, from random blogs and websites. I didn't hear this particular segment, but I've heard them before. Wherever they're getting their information from, they don't provide citation. I don't recommend getting your news from a black morning radio show.

I never did get around to sending the petition to the Grammys. Either I would have had to find a way to print it off and mail it to the Grammys, which would have cost a small fortune at FedEx Office, or I could have sent a link to it to one of the top members of the Recording Academy, via email.

For more on FedEx Office, check my second book, Infinite Crab Meats, in which I discuss a game I invented that involves going to a FedEx Office and seeing how much it'll run you to fap to completion to Internets pr0n. If you don't end up having to refinance your house, that means you won. An arrest for public indecency is instant disqualification.

I did end up finding a link to what may have been an email address for the Grammys, on the Grammys website. I sent a link to the petition to that address, but I never did end up hearing back from them. It may have just been the admin email address for whoever was in charge of maintaining the site, over in India somewhere. If you signed that petition, and you ended up getting email offers for discount Cialis, you know who to blame. (Hint: not me.)

I spent the night of the Grammys that year working at K-Mart. I figured I might get the night off, because it was a Sunday evening, as I recall, and I didn't always work during the evening, but I wasn't about to ask off, because it's already hard enough to work anywhere near a full 40-hour workweek at a minimum wage job, and requesting a day off is just asking for them to cut back your hours to the point where you can't even afford to drive to work. To watch the MFN Grammys? Pfft!

I know at least a few people on the Internets were disappointed that I wouldn't even be able to see whether or not Kanye won, after all that time I spent trying to get him disqualified. This was back before you could easily catch anything interesting that happened on an awards show – on the outside chance that anything interesting did happen – the next day on YouTube or the awards show's own website or whatever. There was no such thing as YouTube, at that point. YouTube was founded on February 14, 2005, and the 2005 Grammys were held on February 13, 2005. We missed it by one day, and I'm not completely convinced that this wasn't on purpose. The Illuminati may have been involved.

Later that year, Kanye West played the Savvis Center in my native STL. I wasn't able to check that out either. If you can imagine, I was still broke as a joke. (If I make any money from this book, it'll be the first time in my adult life that I wasn't broke as an MFN joke.) Trying to get press credentials to cover the show was clearly out of the question, after spending the past year running a campaign to have Kanye banned from the Grammys. Record labels tend to frown on that sort of thing.

I happened to be at my parents' house the day of the show, supplementing my diet with any food they probably wouldn't miss if it somehow disappeared, and my old man read in the paper – the St. Louis Post-Dispatch – that there was speculation as to whether or not I would be at the show. Literally, it said something to the effect of, "Kanye West is in town tonight for a show at the Savvis Center. People are wondering whether or not Byron Crawford will show up." My old man was like, "Bol, they mentioned you in the paper." It was one of my life's more surreal moments.

I thought about going down there and seeing if there was a way I could talk myself in, like that kid in Almost Famous. Maybe I could take a copy of the newspaper down there as proof that people were expecting me to be there and therefore I should be allowed to enter for free.

There was literally no way that someone who works at a concert venue in St. Louis would have had any idea of what I was talking about. They don't follow the Internets very closely. They figure out which acts to book from one of those agencies that charge artists money to put their names on a list that's sent out to venues, a sort of hipster music catalog for the flyover states.

I go backstage at some of the shows here in the STL to see if I can get any free alcohol from rappers I know via the Internets, and the people who work there have no idea who I am. They think I'm there to steal someone's laptop. They're already wary of having too many black people around, for insurance reasons. The staff at a venue called the Firebird, on Olive St., is particularly egregious.

3
I Gave You Fair Warning

MTV has had its own issues over the years letting black guys into the building.

There was that time when Redman and Method Man were on TRL with Britney Spears, back when she was still about something. Method Man was checking out Britney's ass, and there may have even been some light frotteurism. Britney Spears hasn't been quite right ever since.

Remember when she shaved her head bald and pulled a Walter Sobchak on that car?

Part of the reason Viacom bought BET back in the early 2000s was so that MTV wouldn't have to bring any more black people around than they absolutely had to, to make sure the bathrooms were clean, the vending machines were stocked and to promote the occasional Fast and the Furious movie.

Kanye West was the rare exception. He would turn up on MTV every now and again even before he hit it big. I think he'd just hang out in the street outside the studio and they'd let him come up and go on air, because he looked like the kind of black guy who didn't pose much of a threat, and they needed to have a black guy on air every now and again, lest people start asking questions.

When The College Dropout blew up, Kanye was given his own MTV special, All Eyes on Kanye West. In it, Kanye sat in a dark room surrounded by some of the paintings he did in high school and spoke of the problem hip-hop supposedly has with homophobia. It was one of the more bizarre things I've seen on MTV, right up there with that time Mariah Carey showed up to TRL in her underwear, with that ice cream cart, talking about how everyone needs a little therapy every now and then.

This MTV special may have been in response to any number of posts on my blog in which I suggested that Kanye was on the DL, that I didn't find his wardrobe sufficiently masculine and that him and John Legend might be bufuing. The one on him and John Legend even made it into the print version of the article on me in the paper here in St. Louis. I might still have a copy in my garage somewhere along with my college diploma. Stop by some time and we'll have a look.

Kanye West has addressed me personally on a number of occasions, in interviews with websites, on the radio and even in songs. He didn't refer to me by name, but I knew he was talking about me because he mentioned things that he knew only I would know about. Kanye and I have a relationship not unlike the one Sirhan Sirhan has with the CIA. He sends me messages. No homo.

The success of The College Dropout kicked off an era in which it seemed like hip-hop might be turning gay. There was a series of unfortunate events, including the time Lil Wayne kissed Baby on the mouth at a wedding, the time Pastor Ma$e got caught cruising for tranny hookers, that video of Beanie Sigel trying to shove his tongue in Peedi Crakk's ear and that video of Lil Cease giving a room full of guys the "whirly bird." All of this shit hit the Internets in like a one-year span, and the hip-hop community struggled to make sense of it.

I speculated that increased fatherless in the black community, due in part to the prison-industrial complex, was leading to increased levels of homosexuality amongst young black men, who lacked a strong male influence in the home to steer them in the right direction when, say, they wanted to go to school wearing a cape and a t-shirt with a picture of their own face on it. And that's not to mention the number of guys who made it to adulthood straight only to have their manhood snatched away from them in the pokey. For this I was declared "perhaps the most offensive asshole on earth" by Gawker.

While it's not politically correct to suggest that someone who was born straight can somehow become gay, the fact of the matter is that we don't know how and why people become gay. Certainly we don't know why people become gay. LOL

One theory I've read involves the mother having too much testosterone in her system while the child is in utero. Which is all the more reason to avoid having sex with women who aren't sufficiently feminine. A girl with short hair might otherwise be suitable for a boink, but you have to ask yourself, Could this girl have a decent haircut if she wanted to? If you're gonna make sweet, passionate love to a girl who kinda looks like a guy, I'd definitely wrap it up, but first I'd take a close look at my options.

Many gay people, ironically enough, are just as hostile to science as creationists and global warming deniers, who tend to be homophobes. They don't want to believe that a straight man can all of a sudden become gay, not because they've got scientific proof but because they've got their fingers in their ears and they don't want to hear it.

In fact, some gay guys claim to have once been straight, including guys who were "tampered with" when they were kids, guys who took it up the coat in the pokey and guys who just plain got tired of the hassle of trying to talk a woman into doing the nasty – because gay guys don't have to sweat doing all of that lying, wasting time and spending money just to have sex.

As discussed in the movie True Romance, some guys who fuck other guys in prison find when they get out that a woman's vagine just isn't tight enough anymore. That's sorta like becoming gay, except that I guess you can also fuck a woman in her ass... again, if you can talk her into it. (I'm officially against "surprise anal sex.")

The war on drugs and the prison-industrial complex have had a disproportionate impact on the black community in general and black men in particular. Black women haven't been hit as hard as black men, except that having so many brothers in and out of jail makes it that much more difficult for them to find a mate. It's hard enough to find a job when all you've done is get an education and buy a suit, let alone when you've been convicted of a felony, and that's what black women are looking for: a brother with a check.

When black women say they can't find a man, they don't mean that they can't find a black guy in the ghetto... which would be like not being able to find sand at the beach. What they mean is that they can't find a guy who makes at least twice as much money as they do, to help pay down some of this credit card debt. This weave don't buy itself.

If the government could somehow subsidize weave, that would be a game changer for the black community. A lot of the fake hair that we buy comes from Asia, and we know that China is buying up all of the scrap metal from shut down factories in places like Detroit. I can envision a sort of human hair equivalent of what's known in global geopolitics as the petrodollar, and in fact, it just occurred to me that I'll be old enough to run for president in 2016 – I might have to run with this.

But I digress.

Another reason black women aren't hit as hard by the prison-industrial complex is that black women are allowed to get away with crime. This should be obvious to anyone who checks World Star Hip Hop every day of the week, first thing in the morning, like I do. There must be four girl fights for every one guy fight, and yet who ever heard of a girl going to jail for fighting? Similarly, black women involved in drug dealing are oftentimes allowed to go free, given the opportunity to snitch, or receive a relatively light sentence, especially if they have kids.

This is not so much because the government favors black women, who can be difficult to get along with (hence the fighting), but because it's cheaper to allow black women to be free to commit crimes and raise their children than it is to lock them up and then have to house and feed their kids. That check you get to take in a foster kid is a better check than the one you get to feed your own kid, and in fact, taking in a few foster kids can be a good hustle for someone who has no other legal means to make money – so, most of us.

There was an article in the New York Times a while back about "victims" of mugshot websites, of which there are no real victims. In it, a black chick claimed to have been unjustly arrested at least twice, once for getting into a fight with a boyfriend and once for living with a guy who sold drugs.

I can't speak on the fight with the boyfriend, other than to say that I've never seen an episode of COPS in which the police were called to investigate a domestic violence incident and ended up arresting the girl. It makes me wonder if the guy even threw a punch. I know at least two guys who used to get beat up by women, and ironically, both of them are large, large brothers.

As far as the living with a guy who sold drugs is concerned, here's a translation: "My boyfriend and I were selling drugs. 5-0 raided our crib, arrested us and took our stash. I told the police where the shit came from and got out, while my boyfriend is still in jail to this day, and now I want my mugshot removed from the Internets so I can get a job running a daycare center. Why, oh why, can't I find a decent man?"

Have I read too much fiction, or is this how it happens?

Now the guy's destined to spend the rest of his life in and out of the pokey, where forcible, non-consensual lovemaking is the order of the day. In some places it's not even a crime. If you check what the law actually says, which is something I recommend all guys do, just in case, it usually says that you're not allowed to have forcible intercourse with a woman without her consent. You can forcibly, non-consensually eff a guy in the a all day long, and in fact, some will argue that if the guy's just gonna allow you to, then that's what he gets. He should at least try to clinch his butt cheeks or something.

Rape laws are often interpreted – by people who have no idea what the law actually says – to mean any number of things, including sex with a woman who is drunk, which leads to no small amount of consternation on the Internets when a girl gets drunk, has sex with a guy, and decides the next day that she probably shouldn't have, and therefore someone's gonna have to pay.

5-0 is called to investigate, don't find anything other than two drunk kids having sex, and refuse to prosecute. They're both pissed that you wasted their time with this BS, when they could be out fighting real crime (or at least having a doughnut), and also jealous of the guy – especially if it's a situation where the alleged crime wasn't videotaped. They're half-tempted to arrest the girl just for calling. Also, what was she wearing? In feminism this is known as teh rape culture.

Man on man rape was included in St. Louis city crime stats for the first time ever in 2K13. It was a very sentimental moment, and it resulted in an over 100% increase in reported rapes over the previous year. This means that more guys get raped than women. And presumably, none of the man on man rapes were "date rape." I'd also argue that a man is less likely to report rape – because of the stigma – than a woman, who's not only encouraged to report a rape, regardless of whether or not it happened, but given a hundred dollars to write about if for XOJane.

IT HAPPENED TO ME: I can't not read a first person account of an alleged rape on XOJane. I'm beginning to feel like I'm the one who's the victim.

I don't know why the city of St. Louis didn't just exclude man on man rape from their crime stats. Do they not want people to move to the city? If it's a matter of the law changing to where it's now illegal to rape another guy, which I remain on the fence about (but not because it would impede my lifestyle in any way, natch), they still could have just left it out of the stats. Who gives a shit! Don't all cities juice the crime stats?

Crime stats in the STL are already artificially high because it's only counting St. Louis city, where relatively few people live if they have any choice in the matter. It's like reporting the crime stats of Camden, NJ, where they don't even have any police, as the crime stats of Philadelphia. And it's stuck that way, because why would the rest of St. Louis want to be (statistically) associated with the shitty, high crime part?

One thing they might consider is just changing the damn name. Why not just call the rest of the area, which is not as high crime, St. Louis, and they can give the inner city a new name, say, Camden, MO? That's something else I might have to keep in mind for 2016.

When sagging your pants first became a trend, when I was in elementary school, it was thought that it was because you're not allowed to wear a belt in prison, because you might hang yourself with it. I was told by an older black guy who'd probably done time – he had a few not particularly well done tattoos – that it was really a signal that you're DTF. This was either the late '80s or the very early '90s. I can't remember anymore. My brain is beginning to grow a thin candy shell. At any rate, it was pre-Jersey Shore. He didn't actually use the term DTF.

Fleece "Booty Warrior" Johnson didn't speak on the purpose of sagging your pants, in the legendary episode of MSNBC's Lockup in which he defined the logic of sex laws in the pokey, but he did say that if a guy like him saw you sagging your pants, he'd be in your ass. Imagine when he gets out and sees how brothers in the ghetto are wearing their pants now.

He might actually get out in 2014. He's up for parole. Even if he doesn't – if, say, the parole board has seen the video of him discussing his love of a man's ass on YouTube – they have to let him out some time in the next five years. He was sentenced to 30 years, for a litany of offenses, back in 1989, which, amazingly, was already 25 years ago. The fact that they've kept him this long is a testament to the threat he poses. I'm seriously considering buying stock in a company that makes belts.

Consuming too many soy products can lead to increased estrogen levels in men. An article I read said that increased estrogen levels can cause boys to be gay and girls to reach puberty at an early age. That's why I don't bother with very many soy products, other than soy sauce on my Chinese. Hopefully the sheer amount of fat in Chinese food will stimulate testosterone production and counteract the effects of the soy sauce. There's more food than there is sauce, even if you get one of those boxes of shrimp fried rice with only four shrimp in it. Damn Chinese think they're slick.

A lot of aging baby boomer types are switching to soy milk in their cereal because it's supposed to be healthier for you than real milk, which has a lot of fat in it (except for maybe skim milk, which doesn't really count as milk), but I read in the Guardian – a more accurate newspaper than we get here in the States – that eating fat is not what makes you fat, it's the sugar. Ironically, soy milk has sugar in it, to cover up the fact that it's gross and doesn't really taste like milk.

The puberty thing is obviously true and well-documented. Girls are reaching puberty earlier across the board, and black girls are reaching puberty even earlier, due to percentage body fat. It's the same reason gymnasts reach puberty later. You gotta have a certain amount of flab in order for it to kick in, or else it'll be delayed until you're old enough to legally have sex with R. Kelly. Or maybe even indefinitely. I'm not sure. I find it easier to just assume that all girls with squeaky voices are off-limits.

Because of early onset puberty, some black girls peak early and go on to lead lives of romantic dysfunction. But of course I would never suggest that there should be a different age of consent for black girls, which might actually help to cut down on rates of unmarried black women and out of wedlock births, and thus might even help fix the economy. Not all miracle cures are worth pursuing. It's like an anti-depressant that makes it so that you can't pop a rod: you might just have to run the risk of going off on someone at work.

Social mores in the hood do in fact differ wildly from the mainstream. A blind eye is often turned to behavior that would be viewed elsewhere as, at best, deviant, including sexual relationships between older men and underage girls, which is sometimes cited in discussions of the aforementioned R. Kelly a/k/a Arruh's many transgressions; consensual group sex between a girl and umpteen guys, which is known as running a train (Trizz Nathaniel, to you); and child labor of the sexual variety, which as the saying goes, is wrong on so many levels.

Every now and again you'll hear a story about a black mother who got caught functioning as a pimp for her teenage daughter. Some mother-daughter teams travel for big sporting events, like the Super Bowl and the NCAA Tournament, and book a room in a nearby Econo Lodge. The mom would sell her own pussy, but she knows it has relatively little value. She can't let the girl travel by herself, because what if something bad happens (LOL), or the girl spends all weekend holed up in the motel watching a John Hughes marathon on the Superstation?

A little rain outside is no excuse.

Old white perverts prey on girls like this the same way they do Asian girls in places like Thailand and the Philippines. It costs less than traveling – though a 15 year-old black chick in the US is essentially a grown-ass woman, whereas a girl the same age in Southeast Asia somewhere might still appear to be a child. They're not carrying a sufficient amount of body fat. If they're drinking real milk, they might consider switching to soy. The sugar will fatten them up, and the estrogen will make them even more feminine than an Asian girl already is, if that's possible. Isn't that where soy comes from anyway?

Black girls who are led by their own mothers into sex work tend to be clustered in that early high school age range, same as R. Kelly's girlfriends. They're kids more so in terms of mental capability than physical form. Black people aren't gonna allow a legit child to engage in that kind of behavior, because that's just wrong. So it's not necessarily a complete lack of morals at work here, just a difference of opinion on at what age a child should start chipping in on the light bill.

I've also noticed that the last several cases of underage girls caught using fake IDs to appear in pron films on sites like BangBros, Reality Kings and World Star have all involved black chicks. Obviously white chicks invented this, but it's probably been a while since any of them did it. Otherwise it would be all over the news, and not just in the Florida equivalent of the Village Voice – which, ironically, is where a lot of these girls offer their services.

Someone from a newspaper called the Gay Blade must have googled "Kanye + gay" and found my blog, where on the first page that day was both a post I'd done on Kanye's MTV special and a post in which I threatened to beat my roommate's dog to within an inch of its life and then leave it propped up against a fence along a rural highway like a gay scarecrow.

We used to joke that my roommate's dog was gay, because it had a sort of feminine demeanor and it didn't seem to have a whole lot of scrap in it. It probably wouldn't have been able to defend itself against tougher dogs, down in the ghetto. When you had to talk down to it, to "put it on notice," it would mostly just shrink away from you and whimper.

In some ways it was a fairly impressive dog. It was a purebred boxer, and it was good-looking. It wouldn't have lasted a week in dog prison, i.e. Kennelwood Village. It cost a shedload of money, but someone told my roommate he could rent it out to stud and make way more money than it cost to buy it. Admittedly, that seems like the kind of Four Hour Workweek-style "career" that would most appeal to me personally: get a cool-ass dog, occasionally take it places for it to fuck other dogs, and otherwise sit around all day drinking beer.

The thing is, you probably can't just start a business like that from your bachelor apartment. I'm not sure what the legality of that is. More importantly, who's gonna purchase stud services from some drunk guy offering up his dog up on Craigslist as if it were Kelly Divine's prolapsed vagine? You wanna go somewhere with legit-looking signage out front and papers tracing the dog's lineage back hundreds of years, much longer than a black person can trace his own family.

My roommate never did rent out his dog's "services," but he never got it neutered, just in case. I guess once it got to a certain age, he didn't want to put it through such a traumatizing experience. I went to high school with a guy who was circumcised when he was six years old, and he's still suffering from the lingering effects well into his adulthood. People used to call him C-6.

I believe it was Shakespeare who said that it's one thing to have never had proper use of your schlong, but it's a whole other thing to have had it and to have lost it. Ask any number of young brothers with lifestyle-related erectile dysfunction – you suddenly find yourself with a whole lotta free time.

This dog spent pretty much its whole life attempting to make sweet, passionate love to inanimate objects. No corner of a sofa or a coffee table was safe. I recognized its pattern and started sitting in the middle of the sofa, away from the edges, to watch episodes of Entourage I'd already seen several times before, on demand. (I've spent very little of my adult life working.)

The only respite came when my roommate's girlfriend brought her dog over, also male, and they'd 69 each other. I noticed this one day when we were all sitting around watching an episode of a certain mid '00s-era HBO series. I pointed it out to my roommate, and he took his shoe off and threw it at them.

I'd keep the dog locked in a back bedroom when I had people over, so that there wasn't "an incident," and also most of the time when my roommate was off at school or at work. He'd come home and ask where it was and then get kinda upset when he realized I'd locked it in his bedroom. Well, it was his dog! Where else should it have been?

I'm not sure what all it did while it was back there, but it didn't raise too much of a fuss about being locked up, probably because – like I said – it wasn't the most masculine dog in the world. A straight dog would have clawed at the door or barked or something.

I don't think it wanted to be around me anyway, because it could sense that I posed a certain threat to a dog. Only a year or so old at that point, it didn't know anything about my past, but dogs have a way of knowing these things intuitively. I'm reminded of when my mom told me, when I was a kid, that you could toss a dog into a pool and it would know how to swim. I asked her how it would know how to swim, and she said they were born already knowing how to swim.

This dog may have been aware, on a certain level, that I once killed a dog. And I don't mean taking it out to the shed and popping a cap in its ass because it's clearly lost its damn mind and you're arguably doing it a favor, like in Old Yeller (spoiler alert from the 1940s). No, I once purposely ran over a dog with my car.

I used to live in an area that had been God's country (Allah's country) up until about two weeks before I moved there, and as a result there were small, furry woodland creatures all over the damn place. You could hardly drive up the street without having to dodge anything from a squirrel to a deer to some of everything in between. Some of your shittier zoos actually have fewer animals.

So eventually I started playing that game where you try to run animals over, and I'd keep a running total to compare with other guys who were playing. If there was an animal in the street not necessarily in my path but not so far off that I might hit another car or something, something of real value, I'd swerve to hit it. Certainly, I wouldn't swerve to avoid hitting something I was gonna hit anyway.

This was over 15 years ago now, but I seem to recall my grand total being somewhere up in the 70 or 80 range, and I hadn't been playing this game for a full year when I finally quit. I was maintaining a solid 2+ kills per week average. Animal control probably hated to see me coming. Imagine how many animals I could have killed if I'd kept playing.

One day I was driving down the street near a Taco Bell, and a dog darted out into the street. This was on a main drag not far from a residential area. The dog didn't have any business being there, especially with a Taco Bell nearby. Really, it shouldn't have been out of its yard period. Dogs in suburban areas don't have the sense of dogs in the hood. Dogs in the hood know how to cross at the light. Dogs in Russia can take the subway to a certain part of the city to eat food from the garbage and then take the subway back home. I went to college with people who don't know to look both ways before crossing the street.

Dumb as it was, the dog might have been able to survive if I hadn't swerved to purposely try to hit it with my car. Dogs have quick reflexes, but alas, not as quick as a car piloted by a guy who's racked up upwards of a hundred kills in the past several months.

It's not like I intended to kill some poor child's pet. I just saw there was an animal in the street and swerved, and by the time I realized it was a dog it was already all over. It was easily the biggest thing I'd run over (I knew better than to try to hit anything much larger than a possum, which was already pushing it), and I was fortunate it didn't do serious damage to my car, a big Clark Griswold-style '85 Ford LTD Country Squire.

These days, when I meet a new dog, I notice it'll look at me a certain way. It understands instinctively that I've taken a dog's life, and it wouldn't be worth running the risk of seeing whether or not I'd kill again. I suspect that there's a similar dynamic in the relationship the dog whisperer, Cesar Millan, has with dogs, but whatever he did must have been way worse. Shit, you see what they do to actual people down in Mexico.

In the post on my blog, I jokingly warned that if my roommate's dog were to ever try to go to town on my leg like it did the corner of that sofa, I'd be left with no other choice but to kill it and then cite the "gay panic" defense from the Matthew Shepard trial. I figured that most people would have the sense to understand that this was a joke, because even dogs in Russia aren't capable of reading a blog. Also, it was a reference to something I'd written earlier that year about a kid who was playing ball tag at a party and thought better of slapping me in the nuts, probably because I was one of very few black guys there, and even some black guys who play hacky sack don't play ball tag. Any joke I tell on my blog is just a variation on some joke I already told on my blog.

The gay panic defense didn't actually work in the Matthew Shepard trial, but that may have been because the defendants weren't allowed to enter it as a plea, for whatever reason, not because it definitely wouldn't have worked if they'd been allowed to, especially if the case was tried before a Wyoming jury. This is no shots against the entire state of Wyoming. I'm just saying. It takes a certain kind of man to go live in a state with hardly anyone else in it. This was a good 15 years before they started "fracking" out there, and even the Walmart started paying $20/hour, because there were no hotel rooms there, so you had to live in your car, and there were only a handful of women in the entire town, who pretty much couldn't go out in public without being accompanied by a guy. There was an article about this a while back in Buzzfeed.

Later I heard that the whole thing was a meth deal gone awry. He may have tried to cheat them out of some money, and they had to put a shoe on him and leave him propped up against that fence like a gay scarecrow. His homosexuality was neither here nor there, and may not have entered into it, depending on what he was wearing. All guys in towns where people dress like cowboys look kinda gay, as far as I'm concerned. Was he wearing jeans beneath his leather chaps, or was he pulling a Freddie Mercury? Save a horse, ride a cowboy.

The article the Gay Blade ran on Kanye's MTV special ended up being the first of many an article in which someone in hip-hop was praised for his bold stance against homophobia, and I, of all people, was held up as being emblematic of the kind of attitudes the gay community still has to fight against. Meanwhile, I've never said anything homophobic a day in my life.

Anything I've said that seemed homophobic was either a joke or it was meant as an insult to someone who's clearly not gay, and therefore technically it's not homophobic. I don't believe there's anything (morally) wrong with being gay, but if someone else does, then calling them gay is actually a very progressive way of insulting them, because it's using their own homophobia against them.

Case in point, what I said about that dog was clearly a joke. Who knows if dogs can even be gay. And what difference does it make, when a dog doesn't even have the sense to disregard its own feces? It's not the same as in a species that otherwise has certain standards. My point being (yes, there is a point), if you're going to praise Kanye West for taking a stance against homophobia mostly for the purpose of shilling for Late Registration, essentially pulling a Frank Ocean before there was such a thing, and then try to paint someone else as a homophobe, why would you cite as evidence something that's clearly a joke?

Ironically, the Gay Blade's story on Kanye and I proves that hip-hop is not homophobic, because the one example they could find of hip-hop being homophobic – or the one they used, anyway – was so clearly a joke. If someone were really considering killing a dog because it's gay, they wouldn't write about it beforehand on the Internets, both because dogs aren't quite smart enough to read, and because an animal activist might see it and get you buried underneath the jail just for killing a dog. Meanwhile, people are getting probation for killing actual people – and that's if they get arrested in the first place. If the victim is black, I wouldn't hold my breath.

Obviously, the Gay Blade wasn't a very good newspaper, and therefore I wasn't the least bit surprised when it ended up being one of the very first publications to fall by the wayside when the bottom fell out of the print media business in the mid to late '00s.

If only they'd taken some time out to reflect on the shoddy nature of the journalism they were publishing when I put them on notice back in '05, who knows. Maybe they'd still be around today. They could have advertised a lot of costly consumer products, because gay guys have a lot of money, because gay men are one of the most accepted groups of people in the corporate workplace (albeit on a menial, make-work level), right up there with sassy black women.

As Jesse Jackson might put it, don't let bigo-try stand in the way opportuni-ty.

4
George Bush Doesn't Care About Black People

Having dropped out of college, after spending his formative years trading pron with his classmates rather than reading books, Kanye West is limited in his ability to make political statements. He's just not very articulate, and oftentimes it's not clear if he understands what he's trying to say in the first place. Nevertheless, Kanye became increasingly more outspoken in the years following his debut.

On the remix of the song "Diamonds Are Forever," from '05's Late Registration, this time called "Diamonds from Sierra Leone," Kanye spoke of the conflict diamond trade in Africa. Did you know kids in Africa were getting their arms chopped off trying to dig up those diamonds? Allow Kanye West to enlighten you.

In its original incarnation, which was released as the album's lead single, the song didn't have shit to do with conflict diamonds. Kanye was shamed into recording the second version by a young Lupe Fiasco, a good year or so pre-Food and Liquor, who recorded his own version of the song, called "Conflict Diamonds," in which he criticized Kanye for glorifying diamonds by ordering the audience to "throw your diamonds in the sky if you feel the vibe."

About 20 years prior, Run-DMC ordered the audience at Madison Square Garden to hold their Adidas shoes in the air as they performed the song "My Adidas." An Adidas exec backstage saw the sheer number of the brand's shoes in the building and promptly signed the group to an endorsement deal. Selling out usually starts innocently enough, with a black kid obsessed with expensive tennis shoes. Eventually, it leads to that same kid's long lost cousin over in Africa losing a limb. Hip-hop culture has failed the diaspora by not drawing that connection.

The original version of "Diamonds," eventually included as a bonus track on Late Registration (whereas the remix appears on the album proper), includes what I'm pretty sure is a covert reference to yours truly. In particular, the line, "He write his own rhymes, well sort of, I think 'em. That mean I forgot better shit than you ever thought up." Admittedly, nothing about that line necessarily suggests Bol: I'm the one black kid in America who never once thought of becoming a rapper – or a basketball player, for that matter. Why would I be thinking of rhymes? I realized he was talking about me when someone from AllHipHop asked him about my campaign to have him banned from the Grammys, and he responded that it's true that he doesn't write his own rhymes, he thinks them, which means that he's forgotten more things than I ever thought up, or something to that effect. I doubt he's forgotten more things than I'm about to write in this book.

I checked Rap Genius to see if there was any mention of this. There wasn't, probably because this took place back in 2005, and a lot of the kids who annotate lyrics there hadn't started listening to rap music yet.

Edward Jay Epstein, author of many a reasonably priced ebook about the JFK assassination, wrote a famous article about diamonds for the Atlantic back in '82, the year Rap Genius co-founder Mahbod (pronounced "macabre") Moghadam was born. It went viral on the Internets in the mid to late '00s, when conspicuously reading lengthier articles – known as #longreads – became a trend.

As it turns out, you can't sell a diamond back to the jewelry store you bought it from – like, if you bought it as a gift for your wife, only to come home from work early one day and find the mailman balls deep inside of her – because a diamond has no real value. Diamonds are only rare in the sense that one family – the DeBeers family – owns more or less the entire global supply of them and is therefore able to create fake scarcity. They only make available for sale a certain amount of diamonds each year, to keep the price up.

A huge motherlode of diamonds was discovered in Russia back in the late '90s, threatening to destroy diamonds' fake value and thus ruin the DeBeers' business, but then the DeBeers just bought the entire thing – which should give you an idea of how much money they have. These are the people Kanye was referring to when he went on the radio in Kansas City and said that black people "don't have the same level of connections as Jewish people."

A film called Blood Diamond was released in the fall of '06, about a year after Late Registration came out. Its release may have been spurred by the popularity of "Diamonds from Sierra Leone," and also by a more general trend of celebrity humanitarian work in Africa, including Madonna going over there and adopting a baby (that wasn't really an orphan), followed by Angelina Jolie and other white celebs; an MTV special in which Jay-Z went over to Africa and gave out water to kids with flies on their faces; and Bono's campaign for debt relief, which as I recall, you could support by buying an even more expensive iPod that came preloaded with whatever album U2 had out at the time. Africa was the shit back in the mid 2000s.

The DeBeers family, again facing an existential threat, lobbied Warner Bros to include a disclaimer stating that the events portrayed in the film are fictional and that the film is set in the past. The film is set in 1999. This was 2006. But I guess that was kinda a long time ago, in an age when rap music from 2005 is considered quite literally prehistoric. 1999 is the year I graduated high school.

Russell Simmons' Diamond Empowerment Fund sent a pre-Kanye Kim Kardashian on the Late Show with David Letterman to conduct PR interference on behalf of the diamond industry, i.e. the DeBeers family. Asked by Letterman, who may have also been in on the deal, what she did last summer, she said that she went over to Africa, where she saw what a positive effect the diamond trade has had. This was surprising to her, given the way the diamond trade has been portrayed in the media. Kanye, who's since married Kim Kardashian, continues to perform "Diamonds from Sierra Leone" in concert.

Kanye West has a song about conflict diamonds, and he's also married to a woman who's paid to deliver propaganda on behalf of the DeBeers family. That's like Betty Ford being married to a member of the Coors family. People who would buy a ticket to a Kanye West show probably aren't up on the issues enough to grasp the contradiction. That's one of the reasons it's important they buy this book. The other reason is that I get approximately $2 per copy sold.

Imagine if every single one of them bought a copy. Damn I'd be paid... I got it made.

Kanye's most famous, most important, most accurate political statement took place at a telethon to aid victims of Hurricane Katrina, which hit New Orleans like a proverbial ton of bricks in the late summer of '05.

Due to its ethnic makeup, New Orleans is uniquely unequipped to deal with a slight increase in the price of Miller Genuine Draft, let alone a natural disaster like Hurricane Katrina. The people down there are part-black, part-French and part-Native American Indian – three groups of people known for getting wasted on the reg and taking a nap during the afternoon. Making sure they're prepared in case something bad happens, on the other hand? Not so much.

They're also poor as shit, because so many of them are black, and many of the ones who aren't black are probably part-black, and lest we forget, this is Murica. According to Don Spears' In Search of Goodpussy, as immortalized in David Cross' The Pride Is Back, a lot more miscegenation went on in New Orleans than some of the other slave states, and that's where Creole people – like Beyoncé – come from.

The thing that New Orleans is probably most famous for is being the birthplace of jazz, a form of music which combines African and European influences. Symbolically, New Orleans represents miscegenation. It is to making sweet, passionate love to someone who's not of your own kind what Detroit is to the automobile, or Cincinnati is to a chili 5-way... and that may have been why white conservatives were loathe to offer any support in the wake of Hurricane Katrina.

When the storm hit, many a New Orleanean, if that's what they're calling themselves, was stuck there in the thick of it, either because they couldn't afford to drive a few hours north, or because they thought the storm wouldn't be that bad. I remember seeing a report about the storm before it happened on TV at my parents' house. (Why would I be watching TV news at home? I was only 24.) They didn't make it seem like it would be much worse than any other hurricane.

If you've lived down in New Orleans your entire life, chances are you've experienced any number of hurricanes and nothing bad really came of it. It just meant you had to stay inside and sip your MGD rather than stand out in the middle of the street playing a trombone for no apparent reason – which is what they do down there.

And in fact, it wasn't really the storm that fucked New Orleans so much as it was the subsequent flooding. One of the man-made levees that keep the city from being completely underwater somehow broke, either because it wasn't a very good levee, or because the government purposely blew it up to protect the rich white part of town, depending on whose story you believe.

Water flooded into the shittier parts of New Orleans, people drowned and houses were ruined. It was a goddamn mess. Perhaps you saw it on TV. The people whose homes were destroyed, who couldn't get a ride elsewhere, were forced to sleep in a football stadium, the Superdome. There was only but so much toilet paper in the Superdome, and when they ran out, people were just shitting all over the place. It was disgusting. You were best off taking a shit when you first got there and then just trying to hold it for a few days, which is not impossible.

There were stories about women getting raped like it was going out of style. In fact, there was supposedly a gang of guys going around raping people. But that turned out to be some ol' BS. Of all the people staying there, there wasn't a single rape. There may have been more rape in the city if it weren't for the hurricane. Hurricane Katrina may have actually prevented rape in New Orleans.

It wouldn't make sense why you would want to rape someone in the Superdome, with so many people around, and the smell of shit in the air making it that much more difficult to pop a rod. The only thing I could see is if they transported some prisoners who had been locked up for 20 years, with no conjugal visits. That situation may have been comfortable for them, because it was a confined space and you don't get the sense that it was policed at all. If you can get a rod in the joint, you can get a rod in the Superdome.

But why would they bother transporting someone from a prison to the Superdome because there's a flood? If you're in prison, and there's a flood, that just means you drown, right? That's probably the actual government policy.

A few days later, a reporter caught former First Lady Barbara Bush in the airport somewhere and asked her what she thought about the situation at the Superdome. As if. She said it probably wasn't such a bad situation for some of those people, because the Superdome was a nice stadium, and the places where they'd been living were shitholes.

In her defense, I don't think she was aware of the situation with the shit all over the place and the potential rapes. The Superdome probably was once a nice stadium. Those stadiums make a lot of money charging rich people and corporations for box seats, not to mention the fact that taxpayers pay for the actual building of the stadium. Barbara Bush has been in a lot of stadiums, because George W. Bush used to own the Texas Rangers. Their family is really into sports.

George H. W. Bush kicked off his campaign in the '88 election by throwing out the first pitch at a Texas Rangers game. He thought voters would really be impressed with his form, because he used to play baseball in college, back in the dark ages. But he ended up botching the throw, because the Secret Service insisted he wear a bullet proof vest. He threw the ball the way a woman would throw a ball, thus contributing to his image as the "wimp president" and probably ensuring that we'd go to war with Iraq in the OG Operation Desert Storm.

George W. Bush, who was the actual president at the time (I feel it's important to point this out), didn't seem to do much of anything. He didn't do shit the day the storm actually happened. A few days later, when there were rumblings about the fact that there'd just been a huge natural disaster and he was still down in Crawford, Texas, clearing brush or some shit (which is what he does more often than not – he says it's hard work), he arranged for a photo op via airplane. He had a guy take a picture of him on a plane as it flew over New Orleans.

At a press conference, the president then commended the head of FEMA, a guy named Brownie, for doing "a heck of a job." Brownie, a friend of the president's, had formerly been the head of the Arabian Horse Association. He wasn't at all qualified to run FEMA, and they didn't get aid to New Orleans any quicker than I could have gotten it there myself, if I had access to the supplies.

Survivors were forced to do what they had to do to get food, water and what have you. Yahoo! famously ran two pictures, one of a black kid who'd just "looted" a grocery store, and one of a couple of white kids who'd just "found" bread and soda. I posted both of them on my blog, which may have actually been where Kanye saw them. He was checking my blog on the reg back then, because I was doing a lot of posts on him, and he made coded references to it in songs and interviews.

Yahoo! later copped a plea, explaining that the pictures in those slideshows came from different press agencies, who came up with their own captions. The caption that said the black kid was looting wasn't written by the same company as the one that said the white kids had just found their free groceries, so technically it wasn't racist.

I don't think Yahoo! policed those slideshows very well. I remember when Aaliyah died, back in '01, they ran some pretty grisly photos of the wreckage, which they later had to remove. That was back when a lot of pron was being traded via Yahoo! Groups, a spiritual precursor to Tumblr, which wasn't very well-policed either. If only someone had managed to turn up pics of Aaliyah. No R. Kelly.

Asian-American political commentator Michelle Malkin, concerned that black people were getting groceries for free just because there was an epic natural disaster, called for any looters to be shot on sight. She didn't specify any race of looters, but since white people who get groceries for free found those groceries, she was basically saying that any black people who tried to get groceries should be shot on sight – the irony being that a lot of those people probably would have gotten groceries for free anyway, because they were on "the welfare," as Mo'Nique calls it.

Maybe a week later, Kanye was scheduled to appear on a Jerry's Kids-style telethon on NBC to raise money for the Red Cross, some tiny fraction of which probably went to Katrina victims after they were done divvying it up amongst themselves. You'd almost be better off donating to Wyclef Jean's charity Yele Haiti than the Red Cross. Emphasis on almost. (For more on Yele Haiti, check my second book Infinite Crab Meats.) Alongside Mike Myers, from Wayne's World and Austin Powers, he was given a message to read about how New Orleans is under water and you should give whatever you can to the Red Cross.

Kanye instead launched into a bizarre rant about how race had affected the government's response to Hurricane Katrina, or lack thereof, seemingly referring to posts on my blog about black people being called looters and Michelle Malkin suggesting looters should be shot on sight. It was hard to tell what he was saying one way or the other. Stuttering and clearly verklempt, he sounded like an eight year-old boy who'd been told to reach into his weird uncle's pocket to retrieve a piece of candy, and now he was struggling to tell his mother where the bad man had touched him.

Am I the only one who picked up on the sexual subtext in Kanye's comments? Admittedly, I could find sexual subtext in a ham sandwich. Literally. As if it were a fortune cookie. At one point, Kanye makes a Freudian slip. He says he has to turn away from the TV because he can't stand to watch, but instead of saying TV he almost says teacher. That was the first sign that Kanye was going to a deep, dark place here. It may have been a reference to his mother, who was a teacher, because as explained elsewhere in this book, Kanye has a closer psychological relationship to his mother than most men do.

Hurricane Katrina striking New Orleans may have affected Kanye more deeply, on a subconscious level, than if it had hit, say, Omaha, it being the spiritual center of miscegenation in America. New Orleans is the city Kanye West would travel to, if he were to embark on a pilgrimage not unlike the trip to Stockton, CA, I imagined I would take in Infinite Crab Meats, to eat at the Buffalo Wild Wings where Winter Pierzina works, awkwardly glance at her cans, and drive home drunk listening to "In the Mouth a Desert" by Stockton's own Pavement, where I'd get down on my knees and rub one out facing to the East.

If the Buffalo Wild Wings where Winter Pierzina works were to catch fire, and I had to go on TV as the announcer on a Jerry's Kids-style telethon, I'm sure I'd have a difficult time speaking too. For a guy who's written several books, I'm not the most articulate man in the world. Credit where credit is due: I'm sure whatever Kanye was trying to say was completely accurate. It's just that the only part anyone could understand was the part at the very end, about how George Bush doesn't care about black people. That's why they had to finally cut his mic.

Reaction on the Internets mostly consisted of clowning Kanye for sounding like an idiot, and a general agreement that George W. Bush doesn't care about black people. I can only imagine what it would have been like if Twitter had been around back then. Kanye would have been trending for a week straight. It would have been up there with the Sharkeisha fight video and the video of Charles Ramsey explaining how he rescued three white girls from his Mexican neighbor's sex dungeon. Backlash was minimal, because what he said was obviously true.

Fast forward several years later. Barack Obama was now president. George W. Bush had long since escaped to his ranch in Crawford, TX, to hardly be heard from again. He can't travel to any foreign countries because he'll be arrested as a war criminal. He's taken up making paintings that look not unlike the religious paintings Joe Pesci's mother made in the movie Goodfellas. He must have finally cleared all of the brush on his ranch.

If it wasn't already clear that George W. Bush is trolling us from any number of things he's done over the course of his lifetime, it should have been clear when he started doing those paintings. They just don't look like anything a serious adult would do, let alone go on TV and show off. They look like what it would look like if someone actually tried to follow along with Bob Ross. His father, George H. W. Bush, is photographed every now and again wearing a pair of weird socks, probably as part of the same charm offensive.

As a result, George W. Bush's approval is actually way up. It's not as high as it would be if he'd done anything at all worthwhile during the course of his presidency, but it's pretty high for someone who RUINED EVERYTHING. Compare that to when he left office. His approval rating was about as low as a president's approval rating can possibly be without someone turning up a video of him pushing an old lady down a flight of stairs. Between those dumbass paintings, riding a bicycle and his love of cats, it's even been suggested that he's becoming a "hipster icon."

Naming his book Decision Points was obviously a joke, right? What does that even mean? I guess on a certain level it's a reference to calling himself The Decider, an early example of his trolling. Remember that time he dressed like a soldier and landed in a helicopter on an aircraft carrier in front of a banner that said "Mission Accomplished?" George W. Bush is hilarious.

Matt Lauer had him on the Today Show to discuss Decision Points, to get that Middle America book sales $$$, and apparently he really does say in the book that the worst part of his presidency was when Kanye West said he doesn't care about black people. Think about all the bad things that happened during the (second) Bush administration, and the worst thing he could come up with was some shit a rapper said at a Jerry's Kids-style telethon. I could spend the rest of my life just cataloging bad things that happened to me personally during the Bush Administration.

Kanye had sorta kinda apologized the day before, saying he "didn't have the grounds" to call George W. Bush a racist. George W. Bush said he appreciated that, because he's not a hater. "I'm not a hater," Bush said. "I don't hate Kanye West. I was talking about an environment in which people were willing to say things that hurt. Nobody wants to be called a racist if in your heart you believe in equality of races."

You know good and well W got that line about not being a hater from watching interviews with rappers on his ranch down in Texas. I'm surprised he didn't drop a "you know what I'm saying."

W may have also been trying to tap into the racist backlash against Obama having been elected Murica's first black president. For a minute there, it seemed like he might not last a full term. White people were as pissed as they'd been since the OJ verdict. George W. Bush's interview with Matt Lauer, his first major interview since leaving office in January of '09, took place the same day that many a teabagger was elected to the House of Representatives, after a summer filled with angry town hall meetings. So much for post-race America.

It was also the same week Taylor Swift's album Speak Now hit stores and had the best sales week of any album since 50 Cent's The Massacre, a good half a decade prior, even better than Lil Wayne's Tha Carter III back in '08. Sales weeks that strong, i.e. in excess of a million copies sold, were becoming increasingly rare, with even people who listen to country music either figuring out how to download music for free via the Internets or signing up for services like Spotify, which doesn't pay artists shit compared to iTunes.

This was a little over a year after the incident at the '09 VMAs in which Kanye snatched the microphone from Taylor Swift and declared that Beyoncé's "Single Ladies" was one of the best videos of all time, of ALL TIME. White people had yet to forget, nor will they ever. Even white people who weren't yet born in 2009 understand intrinsically that it was an affront on a par with the transatlantic slave trade.

Bush may have seen the mileage Obama got out of calling Kanye a jackass, in an interview with CNBC a couple of days after the VMAs, perhaps sensing an opportunity to reach some common ground with his white constituency after a long, hot summer of angry town hall meetings. It was supposedly off the record, but somehow it still ended up on TV. Hmm...

Is it even possible to have the president tell you something off the record and then just air it on TV anyway? Maybe back in the days pre-9/11. These days, they could probably toss your ass in Gitmo for airing something the president told you on the record. The president could toss your ass in Gitmo for no reason at all. It says so in the Patriot Act.

They can hold you indefinitely while they try to figure out whether or not you're with the terrorists. But once you've been shipped off to Gitmo you pretty much are the terrorists. Who wouldn't be pissed at the US, if the US kidnapped you, shipped you off to Cuba in the dead of night, unbeknownst to your family and friends, where you have no rights and no hope of getting out, and you're forced to listen to Metallica all day? Excellent health care though.

We don't even know for a fact who's in Gitmo. It could be some random people from off the street here in the US who were just trying to sell mixtapes. Department of Homeland Security closely monitors the nexus between the mixtape business and the international arms trade, because some of the proceeds might be going to fund the terrorists. The Africans who run the factories that print up those fake CDs aren't on the up and up, needless to say.

One of the 9/11 hijackers, the one guy who didn't quite make it onto a plane, looks kinda similar to yours truly. He shaves his head because he's developed George Jefferson-pattern baldness. I shave my head because my head is big enough as it is, from having spent my 20s living in a bottle. My head is bigger than Barry Bonds' when he got on 'roids, but I'm not sure how far I can hit a baseball. Does "fapwrist" have any effect on your swing? Someone could fuck around and put me in at DH.

I'm ready to play... today.

Closing down Gitmo was one of the things Obama was supposed to do when he was elected back in '08, but I guess that's not gonna happen, huh? A whole term went by, and guys are probably still down there with jumper cables attached to their balls. Now he's a good halfway through his second term, in which he doesn't really have to do anything, because it's not like he has to run again.

Given a choice, I'd much rather have legalized marijuana. I don't count legalized gay marriage as progress, because what good does that do me personally? Obamacare is just a massive, mandatory subsidy to private insurance companies, and those free cell phones he's giving out are probably just a tracking device. People who work for a living already have a cell phone, so the NSA knows where they are at all times, even if it's turned off. There was no way to track bums. Think about it. Why would someone who doesn't work for a living need a cell phone? No one's calling them for anything that could be of any actual use to society.

People who don't work for a living are more likely to be with the terrorists, because they have a legitimate gripe with the US, and therefore it's necessary to know where they are at all times. There's enough money in this country that if the government gave a shit about you, it could find something for you to do for $10 an hour (i.e. sub-poverty line wages; what I make from the BGM). The whole damn country is falling apart. They could at least send you around with a roll of duct tape. It's not like they'd just be giving you money, like they give hoodrats who wantonly procreate. You'd be working for a living. And if they found anything at all useful for you to do, it's likely that you'd be generating a lot more money for them than they'd be paying you. They'd still be exploiting you. It'd be like prison, but for people who can be counted on to go home during the evening and show up the next day without stealing anything or (legitimately) raping someone in the interim. That's my bold, creative vision for a new Murica. It's only a few years until I'm old enough to run for president. Start getting the word out.

5

We Don't Mess with Dark Butts or Lace Fronts

Kanye West was once viewed as the rapper who felt the black woman's pain. This was mostly just due to the fact that he had a song in which he seemed to feel the black woman's pain. It's not too difficult to pull a Jedi mind trick on a black woman, at least for a period of time, and that might explain, in part, the rate of out of wedlock births in the black community.

In the song "All Falls Down" from The College Dropout, Kanye speaks of how black women are driven by insecurity to buy things they can't afford and name their daughters after cars. He was probably just talking about himself, really, but he changed the song's protagonist to a woman, because why would a man be struggling with materialism? A man only buys fancy cars and clothes to impress women, to get some stank on his hanglow. I believe it was one of the guys from Good Charlotte who said that girls don't like boys, girls like cars and money. That was one of the realest songs that came out when I was in college.

"All Falls Down" samples a song by Lauren Hill from the album Unplugged 2.0, which also came out when I was in college. I have fond memories of watching that episode of MTV Unplugged with my parents, home on break (like all the cool 21 year-old guys), and thinking what TF is going on here? Kanye couldn't get Lauryn Hill to sign off on use of the sample for the album, or for the single, for that matter, probably because she realized what a shit show that Unplugged album was, and she didn't want anyone to be reminded of it.

If I were Kanye, I would have approached the label about somehow using that sample without having Lauryn Hill sign off on it. I'm sure the label could have used any money it would have received from sales of the Kanye album, since obviously their relationship with Lauryn Hill hadn't been doing them any good for years at that point. She may have been upset, and she may have even refused to work, but what difference would it have made? It's been over 10 years since The College Dropout, and she hasn't done anything other than a brief stretch in the pokey. No Boutros.

Instead Kanye ended up replacing Lauryn Hill with Syleena Johnson, the same chick who later sang on "Down and Out" from Cam'ron's Purple Haze, many a hipster's favorite rap album of all time, of ALL TIME, and also, incidentally, the first rap album many of them ever heard. Used to be, you could find the version with the Lauryn Hill sample on P2P filesharing networks, and I'm sure you can now find it on YouTube, if you just have to hear it. You can find anything on YouTube, provided it's not Prince-related.

Much of the basis of Kanye's progressive image, back when he had one, was sartorial in nature. People who are apt to judge someone's political beliefs based on the clothes they're wearing appreciated the fact that Kanye wasn't as into typical early '00s-era hip-hop clothes, including brands like Ecko, South Pole and Jay-Z's own Rocawear, which are now mostly worn by rednecks.

Neo soul, which "All Falls Down" samples (kinda), is filled with guys dressed in African garb, who don't have much, if anything, to contribute to the upliftment of the black community otherwise.

Cases in point would include Common and Andre 3000, both of of whom famously fell victim to the affliction known as Baduism (there's a pamphlet about it on the Internets) and haven't been quite right ever since. Andre 3000, who has a son with Erykah Badu named after the child actor from the last few seasons of Married with Children, went from wearing sports jerseys and rapping about being a pimp to wearing a turban and rapping about space aliens. Badu also has kids with both the DOC and Jay Electronica and slept with both members of dead prez. Whether or not it was a tag team, I'm not sure.

I remember hearing Erykah Badu discuss her relationship with both members of dead prez in a radio interview back in the early 2000s. All three of them were on this show. It wasn't like the host asked her if they'd all been doing the nasty, possibly at the same time, she just kinda volunteered that information, but then later she threw a fit when someone brought it up on the Internets. She has a tendency to be very open with her sexuality and then get all weird about it all of a sudden.

Years later, possibly over a decade later, she filmed that video in which she walked naked through Dealey Plaza, where John F. Kennedy had been assassinated, but then went on Twitter and threw a bitchfit after Wayne Coyne leaked to the Internets a video, for a cover version of Roberta Flack's "The First Time Ever I Saw Your Face," in which she bathes naked in bathtub filled with what sorta kinda appears to be jism – a video she herself filmed, mind you.

The Flaming Lips version of "The First Time Ever I Saw Your Face" was cool, and I'm gonna let Wayne Coyne finish (on Erykah Badu's chin and down onto her chest), but the best version of that song of all time, of ALL TIME, was by Ol' Dirty Bastard on a skit from Return to the 36 Chambers: The Dirty Version.

Kanye shrugs

Neo soul, all headwraps, dashikis and no real substance, faded quickly and was gone for good by the mid 2000s.

Kanye was brought in to produce Common's Be, replacing ?uestlove, who'd produced the Baduism-afflicted Electric Circus. Both the Idlewild film and its soundtrack shit the bed, at which point Andre 3000 essentially retired from rap. The Roots were dropped from their label, only to be signed by Jay-Z while he was president of Def Jam, where they then proceeded (no pun intended) to set new records for how few records you can sell on a major label and not be escorted from the building by security.

'02's Phrenology only sold about half as well as '99's Things Fall Apart, and they haven't gone gold ever since. And yet they've since released something like eight albums. Back in the '90s, a label might drop an artist who went gold just to free up resources to promote an artist with the potential to go umpteen times platinum. '90s-era record execs didn't even get out of bed in the morning for 500,000 copies sold!

There used to be umpteen major labels, and now there's three. When they began to consolidate, in the late '90s, groups that had gone platinum were dropped like a bad habit. Many of them never recorded for another major label, and some of them dropped out of music altogether. Now an artist can sell in the five figures and still be considered a viable major label recording artist, at least in the sense that they're allowed to continue recording.

Common seems to be on a mission to alienate his white audience. I guess he figures, if record sales dry up he can always act in Tyler Perry films. This began in earnest with his line on the Roots' Things Fall Apart about how only coffee shop chicks and white dudes show up when they perform, for which ?uestlove had to issue a disclaimer in the album's liner notes.

That was the first time I recall this issue being widely discussed on the Internets, and in fact I'm not sure there was such a thing as the Internets back when, say, Resurrection came out. Certainly, there weren't a lot of hip-hop heads on the Internets. People have since gone and dug up other examples of Common speaking out against race-mixing.

"I put bros before hoes. That's the way love and life goes. It's a Jungle out there, but I'm never Fever-in for them white hoes," he rhymed on "In My Own World," from Resurrection (1994).

"Downtown interracial lovers hold hands. I breathe heavy like an old man with a can of Old Style." That's from "Hungry," from One Day It'll All Make Sense (1997).

"Heat," from Like Water for Chocolate (2000), included the following few bars. "State senators, life twirls. Most sell out, like a dread with a white girl."

And the following is from "Real People," from Be (2005). "Black men walking with white girls on their arms. I be mad at 'em, as if I knew their moms."

In '05, promoting Be, he discussed the line from "Real People" in an interview, explaining that for a black man to date a white women went against the whole purpose of having dreadlocks, which, presumably, is to signal that you don't date white women.

Three UK rappers no one ever heard of, Rising Son, Youngun and Doc Brown, all Rastafarians, recorded a response, "Dear Common." You can still dig it up on YouTube. I checked just now, to make sure this really happened and it's not just something I'm imagining.

Real Rastafarians, it turns out, don't believe in separating people based on their race. Some Rastafarians are in fact white girls, and so it would be possible for a black Rastafarian to be dating a white girl who's also Rastafarian.

Bob Marley, almost certainly the most famous Rastafarian, is half-white. His father was from England and came to Jamaica with the navy or some shit, for colonialism purposes. A few years ago, someone on the Internets tracked down Bob Marley's white relatives in England. They had no idea they were related to him and had never heard his music, which they didn't care for when someone played it for them.

For what it's worth, the BBC went to a record store and played the Beatles for a few kids there shopping, and they had no idea what it was. And many a dumbass kid took to Twitter a while back to ask who that old guy was when Paul McCartney performed at some awards show. To think, it wasn't so long ago, in the grand scheme of things, that the Beatles were bigger than Jesus. Now they're about as well known as some of the older black performers at the '09 BET Awards.

In researching the Rastafarianism controversy, I turned up a picture of Common, whoever he was dating at the time (a black chick, obvs), his mom, Kanye West, Kanye's mom and Kanye's fiance at the time, Alexis. They looked like they may have been at a wedding or something.

Common's mom is on the cover of One Day It'll All Make Sense and also in the booklet. She looks black-ish, like she might have "Indian in [her] family," as they say in certain areas. Her hair lays down nice and flat the way many a black woman wishes her hair did, presumably without the aid of a chemical relaxer. She looks a lot whiter in this picture I dug up, to the point where she could probably "pass," if necessary, depending on the strength of her blaccent.

Common himself is also a good shade lighter than he was as a kid. He must have a Malcolm X complex, in which he's compelled to rage against white people, knowing good and well he's upwards of half white himself. He's afraid the black community won't accept him, because he's not black enough, but he's still a little bit too dark to pass. He's a male tragic mulatto.

Kanye West, meanwhile, travels with a suitcase filled with interracial pron.

We know this because one time he accidentally left it at a photo shoot for Rolling Stone magazine. Someone from Rolling Stone must have found it, realized that it was filled with interracial pron and leaked to the press that Kanye travels with a suitcase filled with interracial pron. I don't recall that being mentioned in any Rolling Stone articles I've read on Kanye, but then I don't know that I've read a Rolling Stone article on Kanye other than that one from back in '04, when I was working at White Castle.

You'll just have to take my word for it that there were once articles on the Internets about how one time Kanye accidentally left the suitcase filled with interracial pron that he travels with on the set of a photo shoot for Rolling Stone. I consulted the Google just now, and all it turns up for a query having to do with Kanye and Rolling Stone is a million and one blog posts about how Drake told a reporter from the magazine that he didn't like Yeezus, thinking that part of the interview was off the record.

Rolling Stone is known for printing things that people thought were off the record. That might actually be their editorial policy. Most famously, General Stanley McChrystal was fired by Barack Obama after having been quoted talking shit about the president in an article written by Michael Hastings. Hastings later died in a mysterious car wreck after emailing friends and colleagues that he was being followed by the FBI, but you'd be a fool and a conspiracy theorist to suggest that there's any connection.

In pron, the term interracial is widely understood to mean black man on white woman. A film in which a white man makes sweet, passionate love to a black women, of which there are quite a few (I would imagine), wouldn't necessarily be labeled as interracial. That's just pron. The appeal of a pron film with a white guy banging a black chick is just the fact that it's got a black chick in it, for those (relatively few) who like black chicks. The fact that the guy is white is neither here nor there.

Similarly, you'll sometimes see a Hollywood film or TV show in which a black chick is dating a white guy, and the fact that they're two different races goes entirely unmentioned. Whereas, for starters, rarely will you see a white female love interest for a black male lead in a Hollywood film, even though that pairing is a lot more common "in the wild," and if you do, the race difference is somehow central to the plot.

It can't just be a black man whose woman, whom he loves, happens to be white, because even though this is supposedly Post Race Murica, with a president who's the product of miscegenation, the sight of a black man getting it on with a white woman is still deeply bothersome to many white people. It's the last thing they're trying to see when they spent a good $10 to take in a movie. They might go and try to get their money back. A white actress who let a black guy beat it up on film might have a hard time finding work as the love interest of a white male lead.

A white guy having sex with a black woman, meanwhile, is relatively ho hum. Presumably, the white guy is having sex with the black chick because he wanted to (and not, say, because she's paying him to), and if that's what he wants to do, then hey, to each his own. He's hardly the first white guy to beat up some black pussy – or try to, anyway. If you're black, and you've got some white blood coursing through your veins, which most of us other than Wesley Snipes do, there's a roughly 99% chance that your white ancestor was a guy. Ask Touré.

The exception would be if it's a racism-themed white man on black woman pron film, like the Ghetto Gaggers series, in which black women are called the dreaded n-word, slapped around, and fed peen until they damn near choke to death. Some of these videos are violent and degrading to the point where you're surprised that law enforcement hasn't gotten involved... I would imagine. Max Hardcore was locked up for filming similarly fucked up scenes, albeit with white chicks.

Certainly, there's no way a black guy could film the black man on white woman equivalent of a Ghetto Gaggers and not, at the very least, go to jail, if not end up strung up from a tree. Black man on white woman rough sex and degradation is the pron equivalent of a black man dating a white woman in a Hollywood film: it's just a little bit more progress than we're ready for at this point. Shit, Kanye barely got away with mentioning consensual black man on white woman fisting on Yeezus, which also includes copious lynching imagery. He must be drawing the same connection that I did.

Regardless of your thoughts on whether or not people from different races should be allowed to touch, I often find that interracial pron is better if only because the girls seem more into it. The black guys they cast in these films are packing more schlong than the white guys, which is necessary given how "stretched out" some of the girls are. Some of these girls who pride themselves on being "size queens" don't seem nearly as tough when they're working with a black guy. They're too busy bracing themselves to make sure nothing gets torn.

Some white chicks won't work with a black guy, but not necessarily because they're afraid of being split in two, or because they're not "down with the swirl" in their personal life. They just don't want to be viewed as the kind of white chick who has sex with black guys. It's the same problem you see in Hollywood. If Jennifer Lawrence does a film in which she's routinely worked over by Idris Elba, like in my dreams, she might have a hard time convincing someone to cut her a check for $20 million for her next film. People would have a hard time looking at her and not picturing Idris Elba balls deep inside of her.

In pron, a girl will wait until she's got a few miles on her before doing something super degrading like taking it up the coat or having sex with a black guy. Once she gets to be 26 or so, she's more concerned with getting a paycheck than what she has to do for it. That meth's not gonna buy itself. You see a similar pattern reflected in dating preferences. A white chick who's far too cute to date black guys at 22 might date nothing but black guys in her 30s, in part because she has that much less value in the free marketplace of vagine, so to speak, and in part because she's that much more difficult to please, as a basic matter of physics.

This is good news for those of us brothers of a certain age who haven't won 21 Grammys for songs we didn't even write. I don't look at race as a deciding factor when it comes to whom I make sweet, passionate love to, in part because I'm not a racist and in part because beggars can't be choosers, but I figure the more women of any group willing to let Bol hit that the merrier. That just means women from other groups will have to step their game up if they want to compete. They're gonna have to bring something else to the table other than just their vagine. Back talk and bad attitude will not be tolerated. This is more or less the philosophy behind arbitrage-based sex tourism to countries like Brazil and Thailand.

Over the course of his career Kanye's videos have come to increasingly reflect what must be his own preference in women, if the suitcase filled with pron that he brings to magazine photo shoots is any indication.

An aging, not yet dead Anna Nicole Smith was cast to star in the video for "New Workout Plan" from The College Dropout. This may have seemed like stunt casting, in that Anna Nicole Smith's career peaked back circa Skyscraper, and I'm hardly aware of anything she's appeared nude in since – her body may not have been up to it. The few DVDs and what have you that Playboy has released have just been repackagings of things she shot back in the early to mid '90s. Having said that, she didn't look as bad in the video as she did in the reality show she was in on the E! network, which must have been on cable at around more or less the same time.

I have not so pleasant memories of being compelled to watch more of that show than I should admit to, and not necessarily because I found it amusing. I also watched a lot of that show with Flavor Flav and Stallone's ex-wife from back during the Rocky IV era. Plastic surgery disasters were running basic cable back in the mid 2000s. This was the media environment in which Kanye's mother made the fateful decision to have her tits worked on at the ripe old age of 58 – which is the new 46.

In the "New Workout Plan" video, a hoodrat brags to a couple of other hoodrats that she's become a "video hofessional." She's been all over TV with her ass hanging out of her shorts, and she's invited to ride around in cars with rappers. Sometimes it's the little things. In Nas' "You Owe Me," he offers to let a girl hold his iced out chain. Not to actually have the chain, mind you. Black girl lost indeed. None of this would have been possible, the video hofessional says, without this new workout video she watched.

Impressed, the other two hoodrats want to know where they can get theit hands on this video. The video hofessional offers them a free bootleg copy. Hoodrats are the queens of counterfeit merchandise. That's how sites like Dajaz1 and OnSmash ended up getting caught up in a Department of Homeland Security investigation targeting sites that offered either fake Gucci bags or Trey Songz mp3s. Obviously they were going after a certain demographic.

Fade to Kanye dressed as a perv gym teacher (uh, TRIGGER WARNING) standing next to Anna Nicole Smith, who just kinda stands there and jiggles periodically, when she senses that the camera might be trained on her. A group of hoodrats, meanwhile, run through some sort of maze and do various aerobic exercises. In some cases it looks like they may have been cast because it looked like they could afford to lose a few pounds, and in some cases it's hard to tell – such is the nature of the video hofessional.

Pulling the video up on YouTube just now, to make sure this really did happen, I was reminded that one of the video hofessionals was Esther Baxter, a video hofessional amongst video hofessionals – arguably the best video ho of all time, of ALL TIME. Objectively the best video ho of all time, just in terms of sheer cup size. Though ironically she's never been pictured in a bra that fits, even when that wasn't necessarily the look she was going for. I wonder if that's because no one ever pulled her aside and explained to her that she needs to go to a specialty shop and be measured – YouTube is lousy with videos of powerfully built girls trying on custom bras; I think Chandler Jade once did one – or because a custom bra costs quite literally (yep) an arm and a leg, and video hoes usually perform either for free or at best $50, and maybe the guy lets you hold his iced out chain, as long as you agree to remain in a certain area.

In the song "Wouldn't Get Far," from Doctor's Advocate, the Game and Kanye celebrate how little video hofessionals are paid and thus how cheap it is to have sex with them. As KRS-One put it 20 years before, the pussy is free because the crack costs money. For a generation of women, the attention – if not the monetary reward – received for appearing half-naked in a music video or, failing that, on Instagram has come to replace the rush previous generations of women received from smoking crack. I'd argue that this is a good thing, but I'd be willing to consider arguments to the contrary.

Esther Baxter is barely in the video for "New Workout Plan," but the few appearances she does make are arguably even better than her star-making turn in the video for Petey Pablo's "Freak-A-Leek." Remember the video for the (otherwise forgettable) song "Tush" by Ghostface Killah? Black women felt they were being degraded by rap videos with a lot of scantily clad women, but really they took an L by trying to get rid of them. I never wanted a black chick as bad as I did back in the BET Uncut era. Now I'm back on white chicks. And whose fault is that?

I notice that the camera lingers on Esther Baxter the longest when she's lying on her back with her cans spilling from the top of the two sports bras she's wearing, which still don't provide the support necessary to eat an especially tasty ham sandwich, let alone walk it off. The camera, meanwhile, seems to cut away as soon as it catches her upright doing her best Jane Fonda – possibly at the behest of censors. There's only but so much magic they can show on MTV. A child's life could be ruined. If only Kanye would have thought to shoot hours worth of b-roll footage of Esther Baxter jogging in place, bending over at the waist and whatever else he could have talked her into doing. This was back before Kanye had the courage and perhaps the authority to assert his creative vision. Later Kanye videos, like the controversial clip he directed for Drake's "Best I Ever Had," would redefine the term gratuitous. People of course argued that it was sexist.

The "New Workout Plan" video could be viewed as sexist, not just because it's got girls in it in skimpy workout clothes, but because the song itself seems to suggest that girls should hit the gym to get their bodies in decent shape in order to attract men, who will then buy them lots of material things. Technically, it would only be sexist if it argued that it's only necessary for women to look decent in order to get a date. As a fat man, the real victim in all of this, I can assure you that women discriminate against men just because they "look like shit," even though a women, by nature, shouldn't be as concerned with how a guy looks. Granted, I don't have any money either.

6
Must Be This Tall To Ride

Just as Kanye's career was taking off, hip-hop as a whole was falling apart. Rap music experienced this huge commercial growth beginning in the late '90s and continuing into the 2000s, and then it just kinda stopped all of a sudden.

Record sales dropped across the board, due to illegal downloading on the Internets, but rap album sales seemed to fall off even if you adjusted for illegal downloading. I didn't put together an actual spreadsheet, but you could tell just from looking at the Billboard 200 each week. I used to take a look at the Billboard 200 on the reg as part of the important work I was doing for XXL. This was back during the era of albums like Little Brother's The Minstrel Show. There was so much disappointment.

Again the rap Internets struggled to make sense of it all. Some argued that black people do more illegal downloading, due to our tendency toward criminality and also because we don't have as much money to spend on CDs. But that doesn't square with the idea of there being a Digital Divide. Not as many black people own computers. Many of the black kids you see on Twitter at all hours of the day and night are using smartphones. People who didn't care for lowest common denominator southern rap like Mike Jones (who?) suggested that maybe the music just wasn't good enough. That argument didn't quite hold water once you consider sales of the aforementioned Little Brother album, but I still get a lot of mileage out of it. In part it formed the ideological basis for my legendary beef with Bun B.

Angry black chicks upset with the depiction of scantily clad women in videos like Kanye's clip for "New Workout Plan," let alone what they showed on

BET Uncut, argued that rap album sales were down because consumers had finally grown tired of songs and videos that are disrespectful to black women. To anyone who's ever seen, say, Petey Pablo's "Freak-A-Leek" video, this argument was full of shit, but the Essence magazine set got even more mileage out of it than I got out of my own argument, due to Black Female Privilege. When I tried to argue that southern rap was to blame for destroying hip-hop, there was no special episode of Oprah, like the episode on Nelly's "Tip Drill" video. There's no Oprah for my point of view. These books are the closest thing. They should be as successful financially.

Upset as they were about videos like "Tip Drill," in which a credit card is run down the crack of a video hofessional's ass, as if she were an object, they were also concerned about the number of videos that primarily featured white chicks and powerfully built women of indeterminate ethnic origin, like Kanye's "New Workout Plan." There hasn't been a rap video quite as egregious as "Tip Drill" ever since, perhaps due in part to the fact that BET Uncut was eventually canceled. There's been a lot more controversy having to do with the ethnicity of the models being cast.

Kanye's fellow Chicagite Yung Berg famously declared that he refuses to cast "dark butts" in his videos, or any girls who don't look the same getting out of a pool as they did when they got in. His career hasn't been the same ever since. Detroit rapper Trick Trick stole his Transformers necklace, and Flo Rida almost had to put a shoe on him, though neither of those things had anything to do with the complexion of the girls in his videos. It took me a while to get what Yung Berg meant by girls not looking the same when they got out of a pool. It didn't make sense to me that a dark butt would look any more different getting out of a pool than a light skinted girl would look. It's not like that darkness washes off. Otherwise dark butts would be hopping in swimming pools on the reg.

Eventually I realized what Yung Berg meant, which is that he's not interested in girls who wear a lot of makeup – which doesn't have anything to do with your complexion. You can use makeup to make your complexion more even, but you can't use makeup to make yourself light skinted, if you're a dark butt. You gotta use bleach or something. As was the case with the diminutive Yung Berg continually getting robbed and beat up by other rappers, the comment about girls getting out of a pool didn't have anything to do with the complexion of the girls in his videos. And yet, the two of them were presented together in the media, as if we should be just as upset about the idea of Yung Berg not wanting any ugly girls in his videos as we were about him not casting any dark butts. Meanwhile, I think we can all agree that ugly girls have no value and should not be seen on TV at all if we can help it.

Hipster rapper Wale copped a plea with regard to the casting process for his videos, faced with a similar controversy. There weren't enough dark butts in his video for the song "Pretty Girls." He said he didn't participate in the casting, because that didn't interest him personally. I joked at the time that that was because they were only casting girls. There was a rumor going around. Asked in an interview about the craziest thing he ever did with a groupie, he said he once took a groupie to Denny's – presumably not a truck stop Denny's, with a shower in the men's room.

Kanye, meanwhile, seems to enjoy taking an active role in the casting for his videos… from the stunt casting in videos like "New Workout Plan," with Anna Nicole Smith, and "Touch the Sky," in which he kisses Pam Anderson on the mouth, apparently unconcerned with catching Hep C, to later videos, in which he seemed to be casting girls he may have seen on my blog, which as you may have guessed, I'll discuss here at length, perhaps regrettably.

Essence magazine once asked Kanye where he finds the girls he casts in his videos. This was in the pre-Tumblr era. I wasn't posting as many pictures of hot chicks. He said that the key was to focus on casting mixed-race girls, without whom "there'd be no video girls." He also called mixed-race girls mutts. And I quote: "Me and most of my friends like mutts a lot… Yeah, in the hood they call 'em mutts." Mixed-race girls, as you might imagine, were none too pleased. Full-on black chicks weren't pleased either. They were as upset about Kanye casting mixed-race girls in his videos as they were about him calling them mutts.

Kanye calling mixed-race girls mutts would pale in comparison to subsequent Essence magazine controversies, including one involving the girl who would become Kanye's wife and the mother of his child.

The February 2010 issue of Essence was dedicated to black men, love and relationships. For the cover they chose football player Reggie Bush. Reggie

Bush was dating Kim Kardashian at the time. Again, black chicks were none too pleased.

I was under the impression that Kim Kardashian had a pass from the black community, because she'd been the first non-black woman on the cover of King magazine, back in '07. In retrospect, that may have just been because King was hard up for readers, and they were looking for ways to broaden their appeal without putting a full-on white chick on the cover.

I'm sure plenty of brothers would have copped an issue of King with a white chick on the cover, especially if she had a huge ass, but that would have put it in direct competition with any number of other men's magazines. If they've all got pictures of white chicks in them, what do I need with King? I might pick up a copy of GQ, in case I want to actually read the articles.

Eventually, King went out of business. after the economy began to fall apart in the fall of '08. Its last issue hit shelves not too long after the first black president took office, and that may have actually been what commentators meant when they referred to a post-race America: an America with an economy such that it couldn't sustain magazines with anything other than white women on the cover.

They say that black people suffer the most in a failing economy, because we're the last ones to get hired and the first ones to get fired. That's also true of magazines. Black men's magazines suffer the most in a failing economy, because black women are the last people anyone wants to see on the cover of a magazine. Not because there's anything wrong with black women, but because America is racist, natch.

The one issue of King magazine I ever had also had a non-black woman on the cover. It was Tila Tequila, and this was maybe a year after the issue with Kim Kardashian on the cover, which would make it roughly a year before King went out of business. If you've ever seen a picture of Tila Tequila, it wasn't too difficult to read the writing on the wall. Even R. Kelly understood what it said, and R. Kelly is illiterate.

Like many of the women R. Kelly lusts after, Tila Tequila stands all of about 4'10. And because she's the same age as me, let alone the legal age for sexytime in the state of Illinois, she may or may not be a midget. I had to look up the legal cutoff for midgets, for a blog post I was working on after Tila Tequila was allegedly choked out by NFL player Shawne Merriman. It ended up coming in handy a few months later, when Jersey Shore premiered on MTV – incidentally, the same network that made Tila Tequila a minor celebrity.

Snooki definitely is a midget. I've seen her height listed as both 4'8 and 4'9, both of which are beneath the legal cutoff for midget, which leads me to believe that 4'9 is a bit of a stretch, both literally and figuratively. 4'10 is the legal cutoff for midgets. Technically, it's not a law or anything, but it's the height many municipalities use to determine who gets those handicapped parking permits.

I guess midgets would have a harder time walking from their car to the grocery store, because their legs are so short. They'd be out there all day. And they'd be at increased risk of being run over, both because it'd be hard to see them over your dashboard and because, statistically speaking, the more time you spend in a parking lot the more likely you are to get hit by a car. Duh.

I'm not sure whether or not someone who's exactly 4'10 would be a midget. As they say on Twitter, someone who's 4'10 #midaswhale be a midget. Societies for people who are over 7' tall of course include people who are exactly 7' and anyone taller than that, and therefore I'm thinking that midgets, as a community, must consist of any adults who are 4'10 and anyone who's shorter than that. You gotta be at least 4'11 to be a normal-sized adult.

If you're anything over exactly 4'10, say, 4'10 and a quarter of an inch, you can round up. Only a true asshole would be a stickler about something like that. I mean, obviously they've got enough problems, if they're 4'10" tall. They've got cereal in their house that's been stuck in the same place since the last tall person moved out. Probably something delicious like Sugar Smacks.

If Snooki really was a full 4'9, she could round up and say she was 4'10. She'd still be a midget, but she'd be in that gray area where she's almost a normal-sized person. Real midgets, like the guy who plays Tyrion Lannister on Game of Thrones, probably look down on the absolute tallest midgets. Statistically, there's probably way more people who are 4'10 than there are people who are, say, 3'6. If they could get the cutoff reduced just one inch, think about how much money that would free up. It's the same concept as McDonald's being able to boost profits by millions of dollars by reducing the cost of making a double cheeseburger by a penny or two.

Tila Tequila claims to be 4'11, which would make her definitely, without asinine, convoluted analysis, a normal-sized adult, albeit still an extremely short person, but you can't believe anything Tila Tequila says.

As was the case with Amber Rose, she was once known to be bi, but once she got on TV she hooked up with a brother with a check – in her case, the football player accused of choking her out. Of course swinging both ways is the defining characteristic of a bisexual, but you'd think that a chick who's into both guys and girls would prefer a guy who's not as masculine, someone who could almost be a chick if he styled his hair a certain way and tucked his cock and balls back between his legs, not a burly NFL player.

The night she claimed Shawne Merriman tried to choke her out, he said she was drunk and he was trying to prevent her from driving home. She countered that she never drinks, because she's allergic to alcohol, and the name Tila Tequila is intended to be ironic. I'm also allergic to alcohol, in the sense that one time I drank a liter (not a fifth, the next size up, but minus one shot I gave to my little brother) of Popov vodka in about two hours and ended up falling to sleep outdoors on the way to a party and later vomiting it all up. I wasn't right for two days straight.

Later, I read that a guy in Russia died after competing in a contest to see who could drink a certain amount of vodka the quickest. He did win the contest, so that's something his family can be proud of. Also, if I were them, I'd check to see if a contestant is disqualified just because he dies. Whatever that prize was, I'd say it's rightfully his. What kind of a-hole would argue with giving a prize to someone who was willing to die to win a vodka-drinking contest? That's the ultimate dedication.

Of course I didn't go out and buy the issue of King with Tila Tequila on the cover. Someone from King sent it to me for free, because there was an article about me in it. As was the case with the Playboy with Kim Kardashian on the cover, in which I was quoted, I kept a copy of it lying around my house, in case any visitors wanted to see the many magazines I've been featured in.

One of the very first magazines I was ever featured in was a UK "lad mag" called Arena (supposedly the OG UK lad mag, predating Maxim et al.). This was around the time I was distributing a petition to have Johnny Carson's corpse dug up and left to rot in a wet cardboard box somewhere in the ghetto, because he once told a racist joke on the Tonight Show. It wasn't any more successful than my petition to have Kanye West banned from the Grammys. That issue of Arena came with a free calendar with naked chicks in it. It was for the year 2005, but I kept it on display into 2009, and I only took it down because I moved to a place that didn't have any nails already in the wall, so there was no way I could hang anything.

I've long since lost track of that King with Tila Tequila on the cover. It may have been misplaced in a move. When I did have it. I used to keep it face down on the table, not because I didn't want anyone to know that I read King (hopefully, people would just assume I fap to it), but because pancake face might be my one deal breaker in a woman. It just grosses me out, in a nails on chalkboard sort of way.

Black men are known to be, shall we say, forgiving when it comes to the caliber of women we're willing to make sweet passionate love to. To hear racist white people on the Internets tell it, it's because black men have no standards. The real reason is because it's in a black man's nature to look for the beauty in people, including some people who aren't considered conventionally attractive, while it's in a white man's nature to enslave.

I'd like to think that my own taste in women is more refined than the average dreaded n-word, but apparently it's not, if the responses to some of the RackRadar posts on my blog are any indication. Some guys just like to pretend that all but the five hottest women in the world at any given moment are below their usual high standards, I think. It's an ego thing, not unlike skanky hoodrats posting "thirst traps" on Instagram just so they can dis the guys who respond.

Black women were pissed that Essence magazine put Reggie Bush on the cover because he was dating Kim Kardashian, the idea being that because Essence (not a black-owned magazine, mind you) is geared towards black women, and because this particular issue was celebrating black love, they shouldn't put a black man who's not dating a black woman on the cover. Technically, this was the Black Men, Love & Relationships issue, not the Black People in General, Love & Relationships issue, but I know better than to try to argue semantics with an angry black feminist.

I suspect, based on my occasional perusal of various "bored hoodrat blogs," that black women don't fuxwit Kim Kardashian to this day. You can see this reflected in pictures of Kim and Kanye when they're out with Jay-Z and Beyoncé. Notice how Beyoncé seems to be giving Kim Kardashian what's known as the "side eye." Bored hoodrat bloggers like nothing more than to see Beyoncé give Kim Kardashian the side eye.

This might be due in part to the Essence magazine controversy, and the fact that Kim Kardashian has had at least two brothers with checks (San Francisco, Harvey) while most black chicks will never find one, but it's also due to the fact that Kim Kardashian is one of the first (celebrity) non-black women with a legit tank ass. It was once thought that white people could take so many things from black women, including their men and their dignity, but black women would always have that tank ass – and now they don't even have that anymore, at least not exclusively.

The reasons why black women should #fuxwit Kim Kardashian are as follows:

1) Kim Kardashian has a legit tank ass, and she's probably done as much as anyone – more than the sum total of late '90s, early '00s-era video hoes – to make that look at least somewhat socially acceptable. Anecdotally, I definitely know more white guys who are into chicks with huges asses now than I did back in the '90s, when telling a chick she had a huge ass was one of the worst insults you could possibly say to a woman, right up there with the c-word – and arguably worse, because the c-word is, after all, just a word. You can be a cunt and still have a decent body.

2) Kim Kardashian did a sex tape with Ray J, which had to have been a boon for race relations, and may have even contributed to the election of our first black president. Many pron chicks, who, lest we forget, are runaways, sex slaves and meth addicts, won't do a pron scene with a black guy. Kim Kardashian, a white (-ish) woman who definitely didn't need the money, proudly let a black man hit it on video. The generation of kids who will come of age in a time in which material like that is so easy to access are bound to be more progressive, at least in terms of their pron preferences.

3) If white people threw a bitchfit because a white man who dates black women graced the cover of Time magazine, it would be a huge outrage. We saw this, to a certain extent, with the electtion of New York mayor Bill de

Blasio, who has a black wife who once wrote an article for... you guessed it, Essence called "I Am a Lesbian," a son who looks like he just stepped out of an episode of Welcome Back, Kotter, and a daughter who's kinda hot in the way that almost all Halfrican American chicks are kinda hot. Boy, did racist CACs have a field day with that one.

Kim Kardashian's relationship with Reggie Bush came to an abrupt, hilarious end when Bush dumped her via text message while she was out of town.

He proved to be a more savvy player than I realized. I had my concerns when I saw that he got with a chick who had just got done appearing in a pron film with Ray J. He's in the NFL, and he's attractive enough (nullus) to appear on the cover of Essence's Black Men issue, so he probably could have been banging pretty much anyone. He was at that level of fame where he could have sent his weed carrier to the club and had him round up a few hoes to bring back to the crib. He didn't even have to use any lines. As long as he could still work his zipper, he was in business.

Kim Kardashian has a shedload of money, and Reggie Bush is in the NFL, which means that if he's not broke already he will be shortly, but it's not like a chick won't try to spend up all of your money just because she has her own money; and it's not like a woman would lend a brother a hand if he were to run out of money. That's her cue to hit the exit.

Dropping a chick like a bad habit via text message while she's out of town is a smart move, because you don't have to sweat her showing up to your crib and doing something to your car, like in either Fast Times at Ridgemont High or Waiting to Exhale, depending on your particular demographic. Eventually she'll be back in town, but hopefully she's come to her senses by then, and even if she hasn't you'll know not to park it on the street for a while.

Chances are she's not gonna want to see you period, because she's embarrassed that you had the sense to drop her before she could drop you. If she doesn't have any of her shit at your crib (keep an eye out for women trying to "accidentally" leave shit at your crib), you can pretty much avoid having to deal with the situation beyond that text message you sent.

She'll tell everyone she knows, and possibly also the media, what you did, in an attempt to destroy your reputation, but if you've got a shedload of money it doesn't matter so much if people think you're a bad person. If you don't have a shedload of money, I recommend trying a little diplomacy, but the fact of the matter is, if you're broke as a joke, your image is the least of your problems. Rich people don't need a good image.

The benefit of pursuing a relationship with a woman like Kim Kardashian is that there was never a doubt in Reggie Bush's mind that he was gonna hit that – possibly within 15 minutes of meeting her, in a nearby alley. Not only could he be fairly certain that they'd end up having sex, but he had a pretty good idea of what it would be like. He could study "game film" and practice ahead of time, so he could really put on a clinic out there on the field, so to speak.

Beyond being able to know how to beat it up beforehand, there's also a benefit to approaching girls who you know for a fact have already had sex with black guys. Because some chicks just plain won't date black guys. Not just in pron, in real life! They think they're too good for it. (Pfft.) Some white chicks won't date a black guy until they're approaching The Wall, i.e. like 26, and the pussy's not worth a shit anymore anyway. Think about how many white guys have run up in that before it was deemed sufficiently worthless enough for you to hit it. It's almost enough to make you want to turn it down. Emphasis on almost.

You'd have to think that this was Kanye West's thought process when he took up with Kim Kardashian. I'm sure he was genuinely attracted to her, but then I'm sure he's genuinely attracted to any number of women. I've spent my entire adult life documenting his various interactions with women, so I should know. If Kim Kardashian wasn't known to get more black guys off than Johnnie Cochran, it would have been pointless for him to even bother. Kanye West went to a white high school in the 1990s, not unlike a certain somebody, so I'm sure he knows what patterns to look for. Kim Kardashian had already been in a pron film with Ray J and been dumped by an NFL player. The door was wide open for pretty much any brother with a check to swoop in.

He didn't have to sweat her going back to white guys, because the old saying about once you go black happens to be one of the many stereotypes that's based in truth, and the fact of the matter is that a white guy with a check probably wouldn't have wanted her at that point. White guys, these days, like a chick with a bit of an ass, but not a gross tank ass. And having dated a black guy probably wouldn't be a dealbreaker, provided you don't have one of his illegitimate children, but having appeared in a pron film with a black guy would be a dealbreaker for almost any white guy who doesn't need her for drug money. Really, having appeared in a pron film period should be a dealbreaker for any self-respecting individual, regardless of race.

The Essence magazine controversy, ironically, may have had the effect of driving Reggie Bush into the arms of white women permanently.

The fact that he would appear on the cover of Essence magazine in the first place should have been a sign to black women that he was at least willing to "come to the table." He may have been trying to shore up his image in the black community, particularly amongst black women, for whatever he plans to do in his post-NFL career. He's got the kind of looks where he can appear as an alcoholic, abusive father and/or boyfriend in a Tyler Perry film. But I get the sense that he's what's known on ESPN as a cornball brother. His English might be too good to be fully accepted by his people.

He probably figured he was meeting the black community halfway by dating Kim Kardashian. After all, she's got a ginormous tank ass, she was once on the cover of King magazine, and she even let a black guy hit it on film. Shit, her father helped free OJ Simpson.

After the Essence magazine controversy, and after he had the sense to drop Kim Kardashian, it's been nothing but white chicks for Reggie Bush, as far as I know. He eventually ended up with a chick who looks like a knockoff, flea market Kim Kardashian. That must just be his type, physically, and you can't knock a brother for being with who he wants to be with. At least there's not video proof of where this chick was before he found her.

Black chicks played themselves by giving him so much shit. If he's willing to get with swarthy white chicks with tank asses and loose morals, chances are he probably would have gotten with a black chick. But I wouldn't want to get with a black chick either, after they threw salt on my image like that. Obviously it's wrong to dismiss an entire race of women just because of a few bored hoodrats on the Internets. But the thing is, if that's the way so many of them feel, how can you ever be sure that the one you get with doesn't also feel that way deep down inside? Maybe she's just after your money.

Really, it's not at all different from not wasting your time approaching white chicks who don't date black guys as a rule. As no less an expert than Too $hort once said, you gotta get in where you fit in. You're not the one being racist – they are. If black chicks had focused on trying to present an argument for why he should have gotten with a nice black chick instead of Kim Kardashian, rather than trying to throw him under a bus, who knows.

7
Show Some Courtesy, Curtis

While rap music as a whole was approaching a commercial nadir to match the identity politics malaise that had settled in for the past few years at that point, Kanye's own career wasn't doing half bad. 2007's Graduation didn't sell quite as well as either of his first two albums, and I don't recall anyone really liking the singles, but it did trounce 50 Cent's Curtis in a head to head sales battle that would have profound implications for the future of shitty commercial rap music.

---

50 Cent's album probably should have been released a good six months, if not a year, before Kanye was set to drop Graduation. This was already upwards of two years after The Massacre, which sold well and yet still managed to disappoint. It was a huge dropoff from Get Rich or Die Tryin', but then Get Rich or Die Tryin' sold more copies than Elvis and the Beatles combined. Buhweet wishes he had an album that sold as well as Get Rich or Die Tryin', let alone Kanye.

Curtis was gonna be called something else, but then Fiddy changed the name of the album to Curtis because of his beef with Cam'ron. This was back when 50 Cent still had a lot of self-esteem due to the fact that he'd sold so many records – even though The Massacre didn't sell as well as Get Rich or Die Tryin', and if he'd had Lloyd Banks or someone do a simple regression analysis on his album sales, he would have realized that few people would really give a shit about Curtis, and eventually he'd end up where he is now, not able to even get a release date on Interscope.

50 Cent was on the radio probably trying to generate interest for whatever the album was being called at that point, and the conversation turned to Koch Records. That may have been when Fiddy coined the term Koch Graveyard. Actually, Fiddy referred to Koch Records as a graveyard, I saw it and started referring to Koch Records as Koch Graveyard in album reviews I was writing for my own blog, and the column I was writing for XXL's website. That may or may not have had to do with Koch eventually changing its name to E1 Music.

There definitely was some truth to the idea of Koch Records being a graveyard. They mainly dealt with artists who once had a deal with a major label and had since been given the boot. You probably didn't get shit in the way of an advance from Koch Records, but supposedly you got $8 per record sold. Contrast that with a typical major label deal (even before this 360 deal BS), in which you get a pretty sizable advance, at least for someone who grew up in the projects, but then you never, ever get a check from the label again in your life.

It used to be, you could at least make money performing live. In a 360 deal, it might be necessary to do a commercial or endorse some sort of product. The deals might be structured that way, on the outside chance that the artist has at least a modicum of pride. The label is entitled to at least some of your touring revenue, which effectively means that they're entitled to all of the money you make from touring. If you were to become popular enough to make back the amount of your advance, what they'd do is, they'd hire a buncha people to help you promote the album and then charge you for that. That's how the scam works.

So for example, Cam'ron, for all of his talk about how Koch Records is not a graveyard, was signed to a major label. He's been signed to most major labels. He started out with Sony, I believe, then he was on Rocafella for a period of time, and then he was on Atlantic Records. In fact, I think that's as many major labels as you can possibly be on, due to corporate consolidation, deregulation, the Telecommunication Act of 1996 and what have you. Jim Jones, who can't rap, had to settle for Koch Graveyard. But then Jim Jones ended up having a hit song that was probably as popular as any Cam'ron song ever was – unless I'm forgetting something.

Alan Grunblatt, CEO of Koch Records, called in to the station while Fiddy was on the air calling his label a graveyard. The whole thing was being filmed for later broadcast on the Internets, and he had Cam'ron there in the room with him. The whole thing was probably staged by Hot 97, which was known at the time for trying to provoke shootouts between artists in the streets outside the building from which it broadcast. There was a famous article about it in the New Yorker back in the mid 2000s. The building they were in was trying to evict them, on the grounds that who would want some shit like that going on in their building, but come to find out it may have just been a shakedown. The building was either owned or surreptitiously controlled by the mafia.

Grunblatt insisted that his label wasn't a graveyard and then handed the phone to Cam'ron, who got into a hilarious argument with Fiddy about how his weed carrier Jim Jones sells at least as many records as Fiddy's weed carriers Lloyd Banks and Tony Yayo, and makes more money per record sold. In a subsequent dis record, Fiddy would suggest that Jim Jones is now more famous than Cam'ron, and therefore he should be leader of Dipset. In response, Cam'ron would mostly just make fun of the fact that 50 Cent's government name is Curtis. Hence the name of Fiddy's third album.

Curtis probably should have hit shelves some time that spring, maybe around the time when Tony Yayo allegedly slapped Jimmy Henchman's son. I actually speculated at the time that this was a publicity stunt for the album and declared it one of the top rap publicity stunts of all time, of ALL TIME. Not that I condone slapping another man's son, regardless of the reason. I'm just saying. Something like that is bound to generate publicity. That's just the world we live in.

I say allegedly because we don't know for a fact that Tony Yayo slapped Jimmy Henchman's son. I think it was announced at the time and widely rumored on the Internets that Tony Yayo slapped Jimmy Henchman's son, and in fact Henchman's son identified Yayo to the police as the attacker (stop snitching, Lil' Henchman), but some other guy later turned himself in for it and ended up doing time in the pokey.

It's not uncommon in hip-hop for a rapper to keep another guy around precisely for the purpose of turning himself in to the police and possibly doing time for any crimes the rapper may have committed. Yayo himself was 50 Cent's weed carrier, but 50 Cent – who once did time in a court-ordered rehab after testing positive for crack cocaine – doesn't do drugs or alcohol. The most he might need a weed carrier around for is if Ja Rule tries to stab him again. For a period of time there he had Young Buck, who proved his facility with knives stabbing someone on Dr. Dre's behalf at an awards show.

Young Buck was let go from G-Unit after complaining – if you can imagine – that he never once received a royalty check from G-Unit Records. He probably never got a meaningful check from G-Unit other than the amount he signed for in the first place, which he of course had to spend on drugs, a PlayStation 3 and a car with spinning rims. Later, Fiddy released audio of Young Buck on the phone crying and complaining about how confused he gets. While I found this amusing, I don't feel that Young Buck was fully appreciated, just in terms of his willingness to stab people. Someone like that is a valuable member of any organization.

The attack on Jimmy Henchman's son was supposedly prompted by Yayo and whoever else was there seeing the kid walking down the street in a Czar Entertainment t-shirt. He was either on his way to or from his father's office, which was near 50 Cent's offices. Tony Yayo, et al. may have been out purchasing 50 Cent a blooming onion from Outback Steakhouse. That's one of the things a weed carrier does, in addition to holding any contraband, in case they're stopped by the police.

Henchman's Czar Entertainment managed The Game, who was once sorta kinda a member of G-Unit and had since had a falling out with the crew, leading to a shootout at... you guessed it, Hot 97. The Game refused to join Fiddy in dissing Fat Joe and Jadakiss, who had done that song "New York" with Fiddy's arch nemesis Ja Rule, maybe the last Ja Rule song anyone has ever heard. Ja Rule has been out of prison for a good year, as I'm writing this, and the only thing anyone has heard from him has been that Instagram pic of him looking like the world's most muscular eight year-old. He had to bulk up in the pokey, in case someone tried to "push his shit in."

The Game was never really in G-Unit anyway. He was signed to Dr. Dre's Aftermath Entertainment independently of the rest of G-Unit, which was signed to Eminem's Shady/Aftermath vanity imprint (of what was already a vanity imprint), and then assigned to work with them after 50 Cent blew up, in hopes that some of Fiddy's magic – rather than just the crack dust on the tips of his fingers – would rub off on him. If it hadn't been for 50 Cent blowing up, it's likely that The Game would have ended up just like any number of other people once signed to Aftermath, never dropping an album.

I listened to that song "Dreams" the other day, dropping off a car for my old man, who can still afford Sirius. It's old enough now that it actually kinda made me nostalgic for the mid 2000s, if only because I was too drunk on Natty Light back then to remember how bad it was. I'm pretty sure nothing good happened to me. Anyway, there's nothing about that song to suggest that The Game ever should have become famous. I guess it's kinda fascinating psychologically, in a Rupert Pupkin sort of way, to hear him keep mentioning himself alongside famous dead rappers like Biggie and 2Pac, Eazy-E and Jam Master Jay, especially in light of a controversy having to do with him allegedly photoshopping himself into a picture with 2Pac, but otherwise it has no value.

50 Cent claims to have done a lot of the heavy lifting, in terms of the songwriting on The Game's bestselling debut The Documentary, and I'm not sure what to make of that. The songwriting on that album is mediocre enough that, and both parties involved are marginally talented to the point where, it could be true, but what difference does it make? Specifically, Fiddy claims to have given The Game several songs originally intended for his second album The Massacre, including "Hate It or Love It" and "How We Do," maybe the two best songs on The Documentary. I'd have to go back and listen to a Game album to say for certain, but I'm thinking why would Fiddy mention those two songs specifically otherwise? "How We Do" is my favorite Game song.

If anything, 50 Cent writing some of the better songs on The Documentary may have been important in that it ultimately resulted in him losing his sales battle with Kanye. Because relatively few people went out and copped Curtis because they didn't like the last 50 Cent album they copped, The Massacre, and it's likely they would have liked that album more if it had "Hate It or Love It," "How We Do" and whatever other songs from it that ended up on The Documentary, if the sterling reputation of the Game album is any indication.

In a sense, The Game destroyed 50 Cent's career. But not in any way that he could have planned. The most Game himself could have come up with would have been to physically attack 50 Cent in the street, like he did that guy 40 Glocc in one of the all time (all time!) great YouTube videos, and

I'm not sure The Game could have won that fight. 50 Cent is a large brother who lifts weight, drinks Vitamin Water, used to box and appears to be upset at least half the time. There's no point in purposely electing to fight with someone who's got a decent chance of defending himself, let alone someone who might break a foot off in your ass. This is more or less the thought process behind domestic violence.

Tony Yayo's weed carrier Lowell Fletcher turned himself in to the hip-hop police for slapping Jimmy Henchman's son. This was widely viewed as a matter of him taking the rap for his boss, Tony Yayo, and in fact it came as a surprise to many of us on the Internets that Tony Yayo even had a weed carrier. It makes you wonder just how deep that wormhole goes. It's like the movie Inception. Imagine if Tony Yayo's weed carrier himself had a weed carrier, and even that guy had his own weed carrier. What we need to do is go deeper.

Lowell Fletcher did two years in jail for slapping Jimmy Henchman's son, got out and was promptly executed by guys working for Henchman's cocaine trafficking outfit. This was later revealed in an investigation of Henchman's drug business, and in fact, it's likely that his goons would have gotten away with it if it hadn't been for that investigation. Fletcher's case would have been just like any number of other unsolved murders of rappers. If only Diddy had thought to sprinkle some coke on the ground outside the Petersen Automotive Museum, perhaps Biggie Smalls' killers would have been brought to justice... well, to the extent that the LAPD can bring itself to justice.

Jimmy Henchman was supposedly making boatloads of money shipping cocaine and money back and forth between New York and Los Angeles in music instrument cases. The entertainment company – as is the case with many an "entertainment company" run by guys in and out of the joint – was really just a front for the coke trafficking. In retrospect, the dead giveaway should have been the fact that his rappers were traveling with anything other than a MacBook Pro with some stickers on it and a bagful of fake jewelry.

Alas, any publicity 50 Cent received from Tony Yayo or whoever slapping Jimmy Henchman's son went to waste when Curtis ended up getting pushed back. People didn't like the singles enough, it seemed, to warrant bringing the album to retail and running the risk of it catching a colossal brick, like the three to five albums Def Jam releases each year the week after Christmas, for tax reasons. 50 Cent, at this point, was still one of Interscope's marquee artists. They couldn't afford to take any chances. Major labels make almost all of their money from just a small handful of top artists, to the point where, if one of them can't release an album for whatever reason, the company could be at serious risk of going out of business or at least having to lay off a shedload of people.

Pushing back a release date only works if you can then somehow generate interest in the album, either by going back in the studio and recording a song anyone actually likes or perhaps by slapping someone else's kid. 50 Cent probably should have seriously considered having another one of his weed carriers assault someone's child in the street. Ja Rule's kids can't possibly be any larger than the guy who plays Tyrion Lannister on Game of Thrones. Only problem with fucking with Ja Rule's kids is that Ja Rule has weed carriers who are willing to stab someone, and Young Buck was probably already off somewhere crying at that point, dreading the eventual IRS seizure of his son's PlayStation 3.

Interscope pushed Curtis back several times, eventually settling on 9/11, which happened to be a Tuesday that year, just like back in '01, and was an easy date to remember because it was the same day as the US-backed coup d'etat in Chile in which Augusto Pinochet rose to power. In rap music, because you're dealing with people with limited resources, you want to make an album's release date as easy to remember as possible. It's bad enough that most people get paid on Friday, and albums don't come out until Tuesday. Is it any wonder so many people cop bootlegs? Ideally, not only would rap albums be released on Friday afternoons, but they'd be available from kiosks in check cashing places. I have a college degree in marketing – trust me on this.

Kanye's Graduation had originally been set to be released the following week, on 9/18, but it was pushed up a week, to 9/11, after the 50 Cent album was pushed back to that date, probably because they didn't want everyone to run out and cop the Fiddy album the week before and be broke by the time Kanye's album came out and they figured Graduation would win in a head to head sales battle with Curtis. Kanye's Daft Punk-sampling "Stronger" became his third #1 single that summer, following "Slow Jamz" and "Gold Digger." There was also "Can't Tell Me Nothing," with ad-libs from Young Jeezy and a humorous video featuring Zach Galifianakis.

Fiddy's "I Get Money" did in fact become a surprise hit, especially in New York, the city Fiddy claims to run in the song, and not so much elsewhere, as I recall. But New York is a big city. You could probably make a lot of money having a song that's only popular in New York, whereas having a song that's only popular in St. Louis is a one way ticket to becoming the next MC Breed, i.e. randomly dropping dead on a basketball court in your early 40s. Kanye himself went on one of the big rap stations in New York, announced that "I Get Money" was his current favorite song and then spit a freestyle over it, apparently unconcerned with giving Fiddy a leg up in their head to head sales battle.

A version with Diddy and Jay-Z called the Forbes 1-2-3 Billion Dollar Remix was released. At the time, they were the top 3 artists on Forbes magazine's annual list of Hip Hop Cash Kings a/k/a the Whores List, as my play cousin Killer Mike calls it. Diddy and Jay-Z are still 1 and 2 on the list, but Fiddy has slid way down to the bottom of the list, one spot ahead of an umpteen-way tie for 20th between people who probably didn't really make that much money last year. The numbers on those lists are all just wild guesses anyway based on back of an envelope calculations of what a successful tour and a commercial or some shit might earn you.

KRS-One, in an interview with AllHipHop, the same site that once asked Kanye about my petition, said that 50 Cent is more hip-hop than Kanye West, and then went on to mock Kanye's "Flashing Lights" as the kind of song you might hear in a gay club. KRS-One, who spends a lot of time pontificating about what exactly hip-hop is, whether or not someone can quite literally be hip-hop, whatever that means, so on and so forth, really is the ultimate arbiter of how hip-hop someone is. If KRS-One were to declare that I'm not hip-hop, I would just have to accept the fact that I'm not hip-hop, with the only consolation being the asinine nature of hip-hop.

A few months before declaring that Kanye isn't as hip-hop as 50 Cent, KRS-One collaborated with Kanye on "Classic (Better Than I've Ever Been)," also featuring Nas (whom I've also written a book about), a song commissioned by Nike to promote their Air Force One shoe. KRS, who's released upwards of 30 albums in damn near as many years now, has yet to collaborate with 50 Cent. Though basic logic would dictate that if Kanye West meets the minimum hip-hop threshold in order to record with KRS-One, and 50 Cent is more hip-hop than Kanye, then 50 Cent is hip-hop enough to collaborate with KRS-One. (I believe that's known as the transitive principle.) Or would it not matter, as long as a corporation is funding it?

Given a choice between appearing on the cover of rap magazine XXL or Rolling Stone, Fiddy and Kanye chose the latter. XXL is more authentically hip-hop, in that it covers rap music, but otherwise it's white owned and operated just like Rolling Stone. I remember, from back when I worked there, that XXL supposedly sells more copies from newsstands than Rolling Stone, but that's probably just because XXL caters to the kind of hoodrats who don't have the sense to spring for a subscription. By the time you've bought three or four issues from a newsstand, you could have just had an entire year's worth delivered to your house.

I'm sure Rolling Stone has a higher circulation overall. It also carries a certain prestige. They don't put just any rapper on the cover of Rolling Stone, though they will put all kinds of random white chicks from the CW and rock groups that no one really likes. Run-DMC was the first rap group on the proverbial cover of the Rolling Stone, back during the Raising Hell era, and I can't think of very many rappers who have been on the cover since. There was Diddy, back in '97, when I became a subscriber. And there was Eminem, around the time Recovery came out, who was famously declared the King of Hip-Hop, much to the chagrin of Black People Twitter.

I'd argue that being on the cover of Rolling Stone still carries a certain prestige that XXL just doesn't have. As a black man in America, your goal is to be accepted in places where they don't take just any ol' black guy. You don't want to get with the same white chick who fucked half the black guys in your high school, you want to get in between Brooke Shields and her Calvin Kleins.

Elliott Wilson, who was still nominally my boss at XXL at the time, was none too pleased with Kanye and Fiddy's decision to shun XXL for Rolling Stone. Kanye was already scheduled to be on the cover of the September issue. Graduation, which dropped that month, was set to be one of, if not the year's top rap album. The sales battle with 50 Cent was the talk of the Internets all summer long. A Kanye cover was a no brainer. A Fiddy and Kanye cover would have been even better. Fiddy had already been on the cover the month before, but since when has that been an issue for XXL?

Elliott took to his XXL blog to complain that Kanye and Fiddy had opted to bless the white man with the exclusive. He was upset, but there wasn't much he could do. This business is all about access. Elliott and XXL needed Kanye and Fiddy a lot more than Kanye and Fiddy needed Elliott and XXL. If Elliott were to somehow piss off either of them, it could have been another situation like the one in which Eminem more or less destroyed The Source and cleared the path for XXL's dominance in the first place.

The argument from racial solidarity didn't hold much weight with the media literate amongst us. Elliott himself was merely an employee of the white-owned Harris Publications. (Man, do I miss those checks.) I'm sure Rolling Stone could have found a black guy to work the Kanye and Fiddy photo shoot. Perhaps someone to guard Kanye's suitcase. If they couldn't find someone in the Rolling Stone offices, which is likely, they probably could have had someone sent over from a temp service. Are you allowed to specify the race of the temp? That could be a business idea.

Maybe six months later, Elliott Wilson was escorted from the XXL offices by security, on his birthday. There were rumors that cocaine was found in his desk. There were also rumors that Elliott demanded an equity stake in Harris Publications, and they laughed in his face, because all he did there was insert curse words into articles commissioned from freelancers. That's how Elliott ended up at XXL in the first place: Harris brass offered some black kids equity and then reneged, under a cloud of racial allegations.

If he lost the first week sales battle to Kanye, 50 Cent threatened to retire from rap music. He said he'd continue to write songs for his artists, like he supposedly wrote those songs on the Game album, but he wouldn't release any more solo albums. Then after he lost he reneged and said instead he'd drop an album the same day as every major release on Def Jam, to sabotage them, as if that had worked with Kanye.

As the albums' release date approached, perhaps aware that he was about to lose, Fiddy warned of shenanigans. He said Def Jam might try to buy up copies of Graduation to help Kanye win. Def Jam had been rumored to buy up copies of their own albums throughout the 2000s, for the publicity boost of having the #1 album or setting a new sales record. You could tell, supposedly, because sales would fall precipitously in the second week. But sometimes that happens anyway.

In the end, Graduation and Curtis both sold well, but the Kanye album still trounced the Fiddy album, and it continued to sell well for the next several weeks while the Fiddy album experienced a huge dropoff after that first big week. That first week, Graduation sold 957,000 copies to Curtis' 691,000. It was the first week two albums sold more than 600,000 copies each since Guns N Roses' Use Your Illusion, Vols. 1 and 2, way TF back in 1991, the same year SoundScan started using barcodes to determine album sales, and combined they sold more copies than the Guns N Roses albums did.

Fiddy could have just moved his release date again – either to a week or two before 9/11, or he could have pushed the album back even further – to avoid losing to Kanye in a head to head sales battle, and the attendant embarrassment, but he probably benefited from the added publicity. It's likely that Curtis would have sold even worse if it weren't for that sales battle. Maybe it still would have been worth it to Fiddy personally to avoid losing, since he supposedly made $400 million when Vitamin Water was sold to Coca-Cola earlier that year. It's not like he needed the money.

8
Upgrade U

We all have our own ways of celebrating success. Some of us crack open a tall can of ice beer and crank up a certain film we keep specifically for days when a check shows up in the mail, while some of us get a boob job at 58 years old. Kanye West's mom Donda West chose the latter, and as they say on the Internets, consequences will never be the same again.

The fact that she thought it would be a good idea to get her cans worked on is a testament to the issues women have with body-image. She probably really was under the impression that if she got her rack high and tight, just the way us young brothers like it, a guy would actually be interested in her based on her looks... when she could have just as easily had any number of guys interested in her based on Kanye's money.

I would have helped her spend that.

The doctor who did Donda West's fateful breast implants and liposuction had already killed a few people, plus he had some DUI issues.

A DUI wouldn't necessarily preclude you from being a good doctor, but that shit costs money, and he may have been in a position where he couldn't afford to turn someone down just because she was in no shape for elective plastic surgery.

A doctor should have enough money that he can afford to be driven places. He shouldn't be drunk all the time, in case someone needs him (though that may not be as much of an issue for someone who does tit jobs), but who gives a shit if he drives home drunk?

Driving drunk is not as bad as it's made out to be. The more often you do it, the easier it gets. Statistically, the more often you do it the more likely you are to get in a wreck, or worse, get caught. Still, neither is very likely. People drive drunk their entire lives and don't get caught. Some people get caught multiple times and don't suffer any real consequences. Some people even kill on multiple occasions and avoid jail time. Basically, the only reason to avoid driving drunk is because you believe everything you see on TV.

Old women die from complications from surgery all the time, and you don't hear about the doctors being banned from practicing medicine, now do you?

Notice how both this guy Jan Michael Vincent, or whatever his name is, and the guy who killed Michael Jackson are black. If they were white, would they be going on trial just because one of their patients died?

I've had five surgeries on my right eye, and I happen to know that before they let you back into the surgery area you have to sit before a guy behind a desk and sign several papers stating that you might not make it out of the OR. They ask you whether or not you have a will. I don't. I'm a homeowner, but it's not a very nice house, and I probably don't own very much of it. And the fact of the matter is that I could give a rat's ass what happens to my stuff if/when I die. I don't have any kids (that I know of), so I'm not morally or, perhaps most importantly, legally obligated to support anyone.

With his mom out of the picture, Kanye was free to drop his fiance Alexis Phifer. Now he could go hog wild, making a drunken fool of himself in public on the reg and making sweet, passionate love to powerfully built white strippers. Or as I like to call it, living the dream.

The end of Kanye's relationship with his fiance coincided with the beginning of the Glow in the Dark tour in early '08. His mother was barely cold in the ground. He probably needed some strange anyway to help cope with the grief. I speculated, at the time, that the timing had to do with him not wanting to miss out on banging any groupies while he was out on the road.

He could have just banged groupies on the road anyway, as long as he didn't bring his fiance on the road with him. He could have talked her into staying home, maybe give her a few dollars to go shopping. But as often as he's photographed, it was only a matter of time before she found out. This is not the 1970s anymore. And it's not in a black woman's nature to look past minor transgressions to focus on the greater good.

A few days into the tour, pics turned up on TMZ of Kanye in what appeared to be the VIP area of some club with a couple of girls who looked like they might be professionals. In one pic, it looks like he might be kissing one of them on the mouth. In another one, he's got his face buried in one of the girls' cleavage. There was a lot of winning going on in those pictures.

Kanye probably could have just found some civilian skank dancing near the bar with three girls she works with. Skanks always travel to the bar with a small army, as if five of them are any more capable than just the one. (If this is how you go out, it might be time to pause and reflect.)

It's actually preferable for celebs to get it on with professionals, for reasons of safety and discretion. A woman who does this for a living knows better than to take pictures of your peen and your coke stash while you're passed out on the bed and try to sell them to Media Take Out. The Russian mafia would make sure she wound up face down in a river, if she did.

These clubs have people who work there whose job it is to set you up with a professional. In fact, one of the girls Tiger Woods used to bang was a hoo-er wrangler at clubs in New York and Las Vegas. If only he'd stuck with paying for it.

Tiger tripped getting with random girls he'd meet working at a Perkins near his crib down in Florida. I've never actually been to Perkins to be able to say, but it seems like there's better places he could have been having breakfast, if he's got like a billion dollars. His judgment was lacking on so many levels. Unless, that is, he was just going there for the pussy.

A tweaker I used to work with who used to live in – where else? – Florida used to swear by Golden Corral. I went to a Golden Corral once, back in the early '90s, and I didn't find it to be anything to write home about. Its main appeal would be if you could only afford to eat out once a year (no Boutros) and you wanted to get as much food as possible for your nine dollars.

This chick went to a Golden Corral here in the STL and said it sucked balls compared to the ones down south. So it could be that ostensibly shitty chain restaurants in the south are actually way better than they are everywhere else. It doesn't seem like they should be, based on what I know about how those kinds of businesses work, but who knows.

Tiger Woods was getting so much stank from hoo-ers in clubs that he thought he was some sort of ladies man. He may have been under the impression that eventually he'd be able to tell his wife about it, and she'd be cool with it. Really, she should have been, because he had like a billion dollars. It's not like she got with him in the first place because they had so much in common. Does she even speak English? Have her looks improved since they got married? I rest on your face.

There was a guy who used to call in to the late, great Patrice O'Neal's short-lived Sirius XM radio show The Black Phillip Show who had a small harem of women who were aware of each other and willing to cooperate. Banging a woman who knows that you have other women you bang on the reg, and who's cool with that, is the ultimate in masculinity. Being really good at golf is down at the other end of the spectrum.

In retrospect, the "Flashing Lights" video, which hit the Internets a few weeks before Kanye set out on tour, may have been intended as a sort of preemptive mea culpa.

Directed by Spike Jonze, who does some of his worst work (relatively speaking) with Kanye, the "Flashing Lights" video is reminiscent of the movie The Brown Bunny, in which Vincent Gallo rides a motorcycle around in the desert for a while and then gets a "mouth hug" from Chloe Sevigny – which may have actually been the whole purpose of making that film. If it was, my hat is off to that brother. #strategery

I already liked Chloe Sevigny, because duh. Now my respect for the woman is on a whole different level. I'd wife on GP, even though she's probably in her 40s now. We already know her head game is vicious – and it's possible that it's even better than it was back when I was in college. A woman's jaw muscles gradually grow stronger as she gets older, from constantly running her mouth. Her vagine, meanwhile, dries up, begins to smell like moth balls and no longer serves a biological purpose.

In the video, a Mustang pulls up to a remote location in a desert. Out hops a tall model in underwear and a fur coat. She walks towards the camera, rids herself of the fur coat, and then walks back towards the car, at which point we're treated to a gratuitous shot of her ass.

Rita G, who plays the model in the video, has ginormous cans. At the time

I remarked that I couldn't tell if they were real, but if they weren't they were completely acceptable fakes. She later appeared on the Stern Show, seemingly for no other reason than to stand there with her shirt off for a while, for a segment that would later run for years on Howard TV On Demand.

Rita G's cans actually look more fake with her shirt off than with it on. They jiggle quite a bit, especially when she walks, which makes them seem like they must be real, because implants usually seem kinda static. But they retain their shape too well when they're not supported by a bra – even when she's lying flat on her back.

So she pops open a trunk, and there's Kanye bound and gagged. She then reaches in, grabs a shovel and proceeds to beat him to a bloody pulp. But it's obviously just a sack of potatoes or some shit in the trunk.

A second version of the "Flashing Lights" video randomly appeared a few weeks later, on a weekend, when the Internets are usually a ghost town. It may have somehow leaked to the Internets, rather than being officially released. I speculated that Kanye didn't want people to see it because he came up with the idea in a fit of rage, after breaking up with his fiance, then later thought better of releasing it.

In this second version, a model chick rolls out of bed at the ass crack of noon, as if she's a "professional blogger." The first thing she does is have a drink. Later, she goes out and kicks it, stumbles home drunk and is violently raped in an alley. Damn.

While on the surface it appeared to be some sort of PSA about the dangers of getting drunk on the reg and hanging out in sketchy places, I speculated that it may have been intended as a message to his ex, who may or may not have had a drinking problem (I don't know her personally), about what life might be like without him.

I was reminded of Bill Hicks' bit about the dream he had in which a woman who rejected him would see him on the Tonight Show while she's in a trailer with some fat redneck making love to/on her.

I first stumbled upon a pic of Alexis' replacement, Amber Rose, on one of those Show magazine-style sites for pics of black chicks with huge asses. I don't always care for the style of those pics, and black chicks with huge asses aren't necessarily my thing anyway, though I wouldn't kick one out of my bed. But this Amber Rose pic was striking, because she was rocking the skee ball a/k/a the little brother, and while she appeared to be white, she has a ginormous ass.

Those pics may have also appealed to Kanye because, with that bald head, he can pretend she's a guy while hitting it from the back, but he doesn't have to sweat shoving it in her pooper, which is gross, getting mud on the helmet. That is, if you buy the argument that Kanye is deeply closeted. I'm not saying that he is, as I have no way of knowing for certain. Is that a thing for a closet case, dating a chick with a shaved head? The nature of the question is such that we'll never be able to get someone to answer.

Later it was alleged that she's quasi black, the way Mariah Carey is nominally black. Supposedly, she's half white and half Cape Verdean.

I googled Cape Verdean women, and all of the pics it turned up looked like light skinted black women from here in the US, like Stacey Dash, but I wasn't sure if that was just because the only women there anyone thought to photograph were light skinted. If you judged black American women on the basis of rap videos, you'd think they were all mixed race – which they are, but not that mixed race.

So I posted those pics that I found, beneath which I stated that I would make sweet, passionate love to her despite the fact that she doesn't have any hair. I encourage women to grow as much hair as they possibly can, but obviously I'm not gonna kick a woman out of my bed just because we have the same haircut. Depending on how it looks, I might not be able to take her anywhere though.

People always point to examples of celebrities who still look hot bald, especially Natalie Portman circa V for Vendetta, but I'm sure part of the appeal is that you know how they look with hair, and you're surprised they're not completely disgusting. If you'd never seen those girls before a day in your life, would you look twice, if they didn't have any hair, especially if there was another girl nearby who did?

Pictures emerged of Amber Rose hugged up with some other girl, who was dressed as a guy. This may have been the least sexy lesbianism of all time, of ALL TIME. Amber Rose's ass was still on point, but I'm deeply bothered by black butch lesbians... you know, the ones who dress up like thugs in circa 2003 hip-hop clothes. Eww.

The girlfriend was supposedly pissed that Kanye stole Amber Rose from her and somehow turned her straight in the process. I can't imagine it was difficult, though, for Amber Rose, who'd worked as a stripper before she got with Kanye – and not at some sort of lesbian strip club, god forbid. This was really just an extension of what she does professionally.

Meanwhile on the Internets, the fact that Amber Rose was secretly lesbian suggested that Kanye wasn't really hitting that and fueled rumors that she was functioning as his beard. If she doesn't really do guys, he doesn't really do girls, her job involves doing something strange for some change, and he needs someone to pretend to have sex with, to make himself look straight, I can see how that could have worked out well for both of them.

If the girlfriend hadn't been so masculine, Kanye could have arranged a threesome. He still could have, since she is, after all, a girl, and maybe she's more doable without all of that South Pole gear, but there's always the risk that the two girls will start going at it and leave you to fap in the corner.

Rumors began to swirl that Kanye was considering marrying Amber Rose. They may have just been created by the press out of whole cloth.

Kanye didn't address it on his blog one way or the other. He hadn't used the blog to issue very many statements, until the Taylor Swift incident, at which point he began weighing in more often.

He probably had no intention to marry Amber Rose, but he didn't want to say anything, because you don't want a chick you're banging to pick up the paper and see where you said that you don't intend on marrying her, you're just stringing her along for the sex. A publication that would run a story on whether or not Kanye West intends to marry Amber Rose is precisely the kind of publication Amber Rose would read, if she reads anything at all.

I'm sure it would have been all over the bored hoodrat blogs. They slavishly report on any and every single thing certain celebrities do, because that's how the business model works, but they love nothing more than a story about a black male celeb hooking up with a white chick, let alone wifing a white chick. It gets the hoodrats all worked up into a lather, which is good for driving pageviews. They comment on the post hundreds, if not thousands of times, and they send the link to everyone they know, to spread awareness of this outrage.

Amber Rose almost certainly was hoping Kanye would wife that. Even if she didn't have any real interest in him personally – or men in general, for that matter – that could have been a huge come-up. If she couldn't stand being with him long term, she could have married him for a while and then filed for divorce. I can't imagine a judge would have a hard time believing that Kanye West is difficult to be married to. And he lives out there in California, which is a good state in which to be taken to the cleaners.

We know she was interested in, or at the very least willing to marry a rapper, because it wasn't too long after Kanye dropped her like a bad habit that she took up with Wiz Khalifa and eventually ended up marrying him and having his baby.

If you aren't as into his music, the video Kanye directed for Drake's "Best I Ever Had" might honestly be the single best thing he ever did. It might still be, even if you are. It's hard for me to say.

It's not a good video in the sense that it's actually good. Visually, it's kinda dark and drab-looking, the concept has hardly anything to do with the song itself, and none of the jokes really connect. It consists primarily of gratuitous slow mo footage of girls with ginormous racks going up and down a flight of stairs.

It calls to mind some of the sports-themed episodes of a series of pron films called Innocent High put out by the pron studio Naughty America. That could be where Kanye got the idea, or it could just be a matter of great minds thinking alike

One of the girls Tiger Woods used to bang worked with Naughty America. She described having sex with him in a live chat that aired several months before his wife attacked him with that golf club, but it mostly flew under the radar, because guys who fuxwit Naughty America aren't concerned with Tiger Woods' infidelity. Nevertheless, you can see how these things are all interrelated.

The bored hoodrat blogosphere, as is their wont, was none too pleased with the "Best I Ever Had" video. Not only were they disappointed in the sexism, they were jealous of the girls selected to appear in the video. If Drake was going to degrade women, how come he couldn't degrade women who looked more like the girls who read bored hoodrat blogs? So went the thought process.

Really, they just wanted to be degraded by Drake themselves.

Sandra Rose posted an email that was representative of the overall response. And I quote:

"Sandra as a woman I am offended that this is all Kanye West, the director, could come up with for one of the hottest songs of the summer. He should be ashamed of this depiction of females. This video in a nutshell basically says a woman's beauty is defined by how big her boobs are and light her skin is."

Wait, it isn't?

The email continues:

"And Kanye being a black man raised by black parents and Drake being bi-raicial (half black and half white) why are they only showcasing ALL Hispanic girls in this video? [...] Why is it the black men have a problem showcasing their beautiful black sisters? You never see all non-white models in popular White rock artists videos."

A theory went around that Kanye purposely ruined the video, jealous of Drake's rapid ascent, while Kanye was seeming to lose the plot.

In retrospect, there does seem to be some truth to that, but not necessarily because Kanye intended to sabotage Drake's nascent rap career. More so that Kanye used Drake's video budget to pursue his own personal whim, with seemingly little regard for whether that would be good for Drake's career or how it would be received.

There was a famous video of Shakur, one of the girls from the "Best I Ever Had" video, freestyling on the set. It wasn't good, but neither is so much of modern day rap music, and I was hoping she might pursue a career as a rapper anyway.

I googled Shakur just now, and apparently she did become a rapper. She dropped a somewhat expensive-looking video back in 2012. I may have been busy working on my first book, The Mindset of a Champion, and I can't count on anyone else on the entire Internets, who are useless to me, to keep me abreast of these things. No pun intended.

Rapping while writhing on a bed, dressed like a hoo-er, she was functioning as both the rapper and the model, and not doing a very good job at either. Her body wasn't in such bad shape, but she looks way older than she did back in

'09. I don't know if it's a result of subsequent work she's had done on her nose, which looks weirder than I recall, or how she's made up, but she has the face of an old-ass lady... to the point where it honestly would be a deal breaker. Either she'd have to wear a paper bag, or I'd have to hit it from the back. Given a choice, I'd go with the paper bag, because that places less of a limit on what I could do with her, though I definitely would still hit it from the back. #fyi

In the weeks following the release of the "Best I Ever Had" video, I received an email from a guy claiming Shakur gave him genital warts.

And I quote:

"Hey Byron,

I was directed to your site by a friend who is an avid reader of your blog. The reason why I am writing to you is because you had posted my ex-girlfriend Shakur. We both lived in LA together and I wanted to write and tell you about Shakur before all the cosmetic procedures. I knew Shakur when she had full C cups, no ass, and a pointy nose. I would always tell her she was beautiful regardless and that she did not need a breast augmentation, hydro gel butt shots or a nose job, but she kept insisting in order to be accepted in Hollywood she would need those procedures done.

So I supported her in getting the cosmetic procedures. Me being naive I did not know she had some NBA baller at the time paying for her surgeries. As time went on I started getting these puss like blisters around my genitals that would bleed once touched and were extremely uncomfortable. So I went to my doctor not knowing what I had and that's when he informed me I had genital warts and that they could be froze off or applied heat to be removed. Now mind you Shakur was the only girl I was sleeping with at the time so I had to question her about giving me an STD. When I confronted her about it she got all on the defense and tried to cut me off. Talking about I probably fucked some hoe and got it from them. But I was 100% faithful to Shakur for 3 years and never had an STD in my life.

Needless to say the genital warts removal was embarrassing and painful and the doctors said the warts could show up again at any given time and that every persons reaction is different.

I eventually dumped Shakur because she was a habitual liar and I found out she was dating some guy name Charles that works for XXL magazine and that is how she appeared in the magazine as their Eye Candy. I learned my lesson from this experience and any girl I date from now on with an identity crisis or low self esteem about their appearance, I will run in the opposite direction."

Charles may or may not be a guy named Carl Chery who now works for Beats Music.

Before, I'd received a series of emails from a guy claiming he dated Ashley Logan back when she used to be a ghetto stripper at some of the clubs frequented by DJ Kay Slay. This was back when she was calling herself Allure.

He said he had to drop her like a bad habit because she was sleeping around on him with too many guys. Later he found out that she gave him genital herpes. He called her to put her on notice, but she hung up on him and changed her number. Fast forward a few years later, and come to find out she's become a famous video ho, Ashley Logan.

He barely recognized her, because her ass was so much larger than it was back then. She once tried to talk him into giving her $2,500 to go to a party where strippers would pump each other's asses full of silicon gel, similar to how Jose Canseco used to shoot steroids in Mark McGwire's ass (no Michael Sam), back when they both used to play for the Oakland A's, but he wasn't going for it.

I posted the guy's email on my blog, and it eventually led to a segment on Kay Slay's show on Sirius satellite radio in which Ashley Logan came on and vehemently denied that she gave anyone herpes, questioned my journalistic integrity and said that she knows of several other models who have a problem with me. I was pleased to know that several models even know who I am. It's one of the few things Russell Simmons and I have in common.

A mere matter of days after the "Best I Ever Had" video hit the Internets, I "discovered" Shay Maria, one of the all time legends of what you might call the Thirst Trap Internets. Her early work in particular, before she lost that last bit of baby fat, is where it's at. Email me and I'll send you a link.

Her pics had already been circulating via Tumblr, which is where I first saw her. I was checking a message board where they discuss girls with certain kinds of bodies, which is part of the research I do for my blog, and there was a post on her.

I googled her, and it turned up her Model Mayhem page. Under credits, it said she had danced onstage at a Drake concert that May, i.e. a few months after the So Far Gone mixtape dropped and a few months before the "Best I Ever Had" video hit the Internets

Presumably, she was actually paid, or at least selected, to dance onstage at this Drake concert, or else it wouldn't make sense for her to list it under credits. Between that and the "Best I Ever Had" video, it caused me to change the way I looked at Drake.

I still have no use for his music, but it seems that we could have similar tastes in women. (Some would argue that the fact that he has a taste in women to speak of is surprising.) And it makes you wonder to what extent the Best I Ever Had video was Drake's creative vision as well as Kanye's. That's something that was lost on the rest of the Internets when the video premiered. The blame fell mostly on Kanye. This was a precursor of how Drake would come to be viewed vis-à-vis Kanye.

9
There's No Easy Way Out

You hear rumors about a rift between Jay-Z and Kanye West every now and again. Most recently, as I'm writing this, Kanye omitted Jay-Z's name from the lyrics to the song "Cold," from the 2012 weed carrier compilation Cruel Summer, at Bonnaroo 2K14.

Supposedly, Kanye was pissed that Jay-Z didn't show up to his wedding. Beyoncé looks down on Kim Kardashian because she's essentially a pron star. If you see pictures of the two of them together at events with Jay and Kanye, Beyoncé appears to be giving Kim what's known on bored hoodrat blogs as the side eye. So it would make sense that she wouldn't want to attend Kim and Kanye's wedding. And obviously Jay-Z can't just show up by himself. That would have caused even more problems than just not showing up.

Beyoncé seems like the kind of woman who can be made to do something she might not want to do, both in the sense that she's proven to be a very savvy businessperson over the years and in the sense that she came off as very docile in that video of Solange putting a shoe on Jay-Z in an elevator. Beyoncé doesn't have hoodrat bones in her body. She might not be black enough. That whole attitudinal diva routine is just an act. So there must be more to this rift than someone not wanting to attend a wedding.

I suspect that things haven't been quite right between the two of them since way back when Kanye was working on 808s & Heartbreak and Jay-Z was working on the third Blueprint album.

You'll recall that Kanye was originally tapped to produce the third Blueprint album in its entirety. It was set to be released in the 4th quarter of 2008, i.e. in time for the big holiday shopping season, when all of the high priority corporate rap albums are released.

Suddenly that summer, it was announced that Kanye himself would be dropping an album in the 4th quarter of '08. That would have been a little over a year after Graduation was released, so Kanye was due for another album per the usual Def Jam release schedule, but given that this was already the summer of '08, it seemed like a short period of time to write, record and promote an album, and the release date seemed to conflict with the release date for the new Jay-Z album.

Later I read that Kanye was told by Def Jam that he had to have an album for release 4th quarter '08, and that's why he ended up releasing 808s & Heartbreak: It was the best he could come up with in the limited amount of time that he had. He could have just as easily released a collection of throwaways from the first three albums and probably made way more money, but of course Kanye wasn't about to do that. Kanye likes to make an important artistic statement with every album he releases. It's not just about turning a profit.

Def Jam actually has a somewhat different stance on this issue, if you can imagine. Word on the street was that they weren't particularly thrilled with the prospect of releasing an album of Kanye warbling in Auto-Tune about his dead mom and breaking up with his fiance, and they told him the only way they would release it is if he agreed to drop a real rap album the following summer.

Shakir Stewart was a Senior Vice President with Def Jam at the time. Graduation did well for them in the fall of '07, but he was under a lot of pressure to follow it up, and he was facing the prospect of losing his job at the top of '09. When the Jay-Z album ended up being pushed back until well into '09 and then Kanye brought in 808s & Heartbreak for his big 4th quarter '08 release, that may have sealed the deal and thus caused him to swallow a bullet.

If Kanye had in fact released 808s & Heartbreak in the fall of '08 and then followed it up with a real rap album in the summer of '09, as he was allegedly ordered to by Def Jam, he would have ended up competing with his big brother Jay-Z regardless of when The Blueprint 3 was released – unless that album was pushed back a good two years. For a minute there, this was gearing up to be Kanye vs. 50 Cent all over again. Of course the media would have played it that way. I was the media at that time. I would have personally guaranteed this.

Jay-Z almost certainly would have lost. The Blueprint 3, with that horrific Alicia Keys song, might not have fared as poorly as Curtis, but it still would have lost. The Blueprint 3 ended up being a moderate commercial success, but no one really liked it. Jay-Z hasn't had a single unqualified creative success since emerging from fake retirement with Kingdom Come back in '06.

Kingdom Come did fairly well commercially, better than anything he's done subsequently, but it might be the least well-liked Jay-Z album of them all. Some might argue that it's unfairly maligned, and... well, so be it. I get the argument that Jay-Z was trying to kick more sophisticated subject matter on that album, but I find that ignorant '90s-era Jay-Z made better rap music. I prefer the Jay-Z who hates women and wants people to be impressed with the particular trim level on his Range Rover. As if.

After Kingdom Come, Jay-Z approached the producers of the film American Gangster about releasing his album of the same name as the soundtrack to the film. They were like, "Uh, no thank you." They may not have felt that his bars on Kingdom Come were strong enough. Instead of just scrapping the album, Jay-Z dropped it anyway. The live-sounding production didn't quite work. Some people did appreciate the return to drug dealing subject matter, but not to the point where it performed as well as Kingdom Come commercially.

If Kanye produced both Blueprint 3 and his own album in their entirety, and they were both set to be released within the same time frame. it only makes sense that he wouldn't put full effort into the Jay-Z album, lest it come to be viewed as the superior product, or at least beat his own album in a head to head sales battle. I later read that Jay and Kanye recorded an entire album's worth of songs for Blueprint 3, and Jay must have felt that they weren't good enough. Kanye insists they were "phenomenal."

Kanye ended up producing about half of Blueprint 3. I found his contributions to be lackluster compared to their past work together. "Run This Town," a cynical attempt to top the Hot 100 for the first time in his career, couldn't quite make it. Surprisingly, "Empire State of Mind," not produced by Kanye, did go to #1 and became a phenomenon unto itself, played at Yankee games and in the trailer for the second Sex and the City movie. Let's hear it for New York.

"D.O.A. (Death of Auto-Tune)," produced by Kanye's old mentor No I.D., took shots at rappers singing with Auto-Tune, which Kanye had just done on 808s & Heartbreak. I'm sure Jay didn't mean it as a personal insult to Kanye, which would have been weird and cruel even by Jay-Z standards, and Kanye does an ad lib on the song, so presumably he was cool with it, or at least signed off on it anyway. Still, this was maybe the top rapper in the game at the time launching a campaign against a style of music while Kanye had an album in that same exact style of music on the market. It was no good for business, regardless of intent.

Jay-Z, who I suspect is on the autism spectrum, may not have sensed that Kanye was very sensitive about how 808s & Heartbreak would be received, but he definitely was. Not only was there the intensely personal nature of the album's subject matter, but there was a lot riding on that album. The pressure for it to match the commercial success of Graduation was so intense that it may or may not have led Shakir Stewart to shoot himself in the face. Kanye West can't sing any better than he can rap, and he's singing all over 808s & Heartbreak. If this proved to be a problem for critics, Kanye would no longer be viewed as a genius, and I don't know if Kanye can handle not being viewed as a genius.

We got a sense of this anxiety when "Love Lockdown" leaked to the Internets. It was greeted with widespread derision, and not just by yours truly. Even a lot of people who actually listen to Kanye's music didn't care for it.

The original leaked version of the song sounded half-finished, and I suspect that this may have been a preemptive defense mechanism, as if to say, "This isn't half-assed, this is raw emotion!"

That's part of the reason these books aren't edited as well as they could be: I'm too emotional when I write them. It's a wonder I'm able to get this shit down on paper. Really, it's a testament to my financial state.

Phonte of Little Brother, a failed mid 'oos-era underground group, in an interview with Conspiracy Worldwide Radio's Friday Night Live Show, said that singing in Auto-Tune is an act of cowardice. I think I get what he meant by that.

Since Phonte's rap career fell apart, he's been singing in an R&B group with a white guy named Nicolay, Foreign Exchange. I might not live to be old enough that Foreign Exchange's music would be appropriate for me personally, but I can appreciate it on a certain level. They write some pretty good songs. They should be as widely acclaimed as some of these PBR&B acts, like Frank Ocean, and the fact that they aren't might be a matter of heterophobia.

Listening to Phonte sing though, you mostly just wish he was a better singer. Auto-Tune might help some, but the problem is not necessarily that he's not hitting the notes. He just doesn't have a very good singing voice. It's courageous of him, therefore, to try to pursue a career as an R&B singer.

At the time, I had this software I was using to isolate bits of this podcast Elliott Wilson was doing with his wife, for trolling purposes. I used it to isolate the part of the Phonte interview where he discusses Kanye's singing and posted it on my blog with the headline "Phonte says Kanye's a coward," which is kinda true but also kinda misleading. It went kinda viral on the hip-hop Internets.

This was bad for Phonte in the sense that it made it seem like he was hating on Kanye, but it was arguably a good thing as well, in the sense that it got his name mentioned more often than it would have been otherwise. I've been aiding Phonte's career for years, in that sense.

Little Brother were the topic of many a heated discussion back in the early days of the old XXL blogs, circa '06, after they were booed off the stage at some LCD rap summer fest down south, leading to a discussion on whether or not Little Brother was too intelligent for southern rap audiences.

This was around the time when Little Brother's career was skidding to a grinding halt, after the staggering commercial failure of The Minstrel Show, on Atlantic Records. For a while there, having really bad first week sales came to be known on the Internets as "doing Little Brother numbers."

Their video was rumored to have been banned from BET for being too intelligent. This was back when BET was catching a lot of flack for Hot Ghetto Mess, BET Uncut, canceling their news programs and what have you.

Later, Phonte jokingly referred to Canadian female rapper Eternia as "Titernia" on MySpace, prompting a discussion about ostensibly progressive rappers whose views are actually quite backwards, perhaps the all time great example of which being that time Talib Kweli included product placement for Hennessy in his wedding photos, and later got kicked out of his own album release party behind a domestic violence incident, presumably drunk off that Henny.

Three days after "Love Lockdown" hit the Internets, Kanye got into what would end up being his first of many fights with the paparazzi. He may have been upset about how the song had been received. It just so happened to be the seventh anniversary of 9/11, and the fight took place at the airport, so that was less than ideal. Both Kanye and his manager were arrested and then released on bail.

A week later, Kanye announced on his blog that "Love Lockdown" was being rerecorded, this time with less effect on the vocals. Before, there were times when his singing was so off that it was beyond Auto-Tune correction. He must have found an even more powerful version of Auto-Tune.

Having sold over a million copies, 808s & Heartbreak was successful relative to, say, a Little Brother album, but the fact of the matter is that each subsequent Kanye West album has sold fewer copies than the one that came before it, going all the way back to The College Dropout in '04.

I'm sure he made more money from 808s & Heartbreak than I'll make in my entire life, but still. He was reaching the point in his career at which his media presence outstripped his actual commercial appeal. Hardly a day went by when he wasn't in the news, and yet he was merely a 1x platinum artist. Not an umpteenx platinum artist like Adele or someone.

Back in the '90s, there were artists who went 1x platinum who got dropped from their label. I know at least a few people would be disappointed if there wasn't a Gin Blossoms reference in this book, so here goes: The second Gin Blossoms album, Congratulations... I'm Sorry sold [Dr. Evil voice] one million copies. It was their last album for a major label. They ended up getting caught up in the major label consolidation of the late '90s that led to the current situation in which there's only like three major labels. When two labels would merge, the acts with the weakest commercial prospects were dropped like a bad habit. The first Gin Blossoms album, the great New Miserable Experience, went 4x platinum. Ridiculous though it may sound, they were still playing songs from it on the radio when I started driving back in 1997.

Radio stations here in the Midwest are good for finding a song they like and playing the shit out of it for a good half-decade, if not longer. When I went away to college, out near the Missouri-Iowa border, there were only two non-country music stations. One played classic rock, and one played some of everything except country. Imagine a top 40 station with all of the black artists removed, and maybe extend it out to the top 80 if it's a year when white artists aren't popping like they were in 2013.

You could hardly listen to this station for an hour without hearing the song "Life Is a Highway" by Tom Cochrane, who's from Canada. In a sense, he was the original Justin Bieber a/k/a Biebler. It was 1999 when I got there, and that song came out in 1991, so you do the math. (I'll wait.) Apparently, they'd been playing "Life Is a Highway," of all songs, every day for a good eight years, with seemingly no end in sight. It was like the Iraq War, in that sense. Finally, someone called the station to ask why they were still playing "Life Is a Highway" every hour on the hour, as if it were "Semi-Charmed Life" by Third Eye Blind, when this was 1999 and that song came out in 1991. The guy on the radio said it was because a lot of truckers listen to that station, and truckers are big fans of the song "Life Is a Highway," because it relates to their lives.

I hope you appreciate these pearls of wisdom.

New Miserable Experience came out in the fall of 1992, but it didn't really start to blow up until the fall of 1993. It was re-released, with a picture of a car on the cover, and I'm thinking that may have helped people recognize it in record stores, because it called to mind lyrics in the song "Hey Jealousy" about driving around this town and letting the cops chase us around. It was smart marketing, really. Four years later, they didn't have the sense to include the song "Till I Hear It From You," from the Empire Records soundtrack, on Congratulations... I'm Sorry, and it may have cost them their career. The guy who wrote all of their best songs stuck a gun in his mouth when New Miserable Experience started blowing up in late '93, so they couldn't afford to waste any good ideas.

In 2014, Kanye West is not even a platinum-selling artist anymore, Yeezus having shifted only about 600,000 units, despite heavy online discounting probably in an attempt to pull the same trick Lady Gaga used to sell over a million copies of her album Born This Way the week it came out.

Amazon was selling that album for $0.99... for the entire album, not just one song. (I still didn't buy it, but not for political reasons or anything – just a complete and utter lack of interest.) And I'm thinking they probably would have given it away for free, just to get people to install software on their computers that records your personal information, but that was the least they could charge and not have it seem like a scam. $0.99 for an album just seems like an incredibly good deal. (After all, it is Amazon.) $0.01 for an album seems like it must not be on the up and up, like maybe you misspelled Amazon and it sent you to some weird knockoff version based in Nigeria. If all it is is $0.01, why don't they just give it to you for free? They must want your credit card number for some reason.

Also, giving the album away for free technically wouldn't count as a sale, and Billboard's albums chart, the Billboard 200, is based on sales. You could have your lawyer try to argue that giving your album away for free is a sale for $0.00, and therefore your free downloads should count towards the Billboard 200, but I'm not sure what good that would really do you, since Billboard magazine is not a court of law. It might just get you escorted from the building by security. Anyway, I'm sure if something like that was possible, Donny Goines would have already tried it five years ago.

After Lady Gaga's little stunt, Billboard changed the rules of how it tabulates the Billboard 200. There's a minimum amount you have to charge for an album, or else it doesn't count. Otherwise, it would be too easy for someone to come along and give away their album for $0.01 on the Internets, get over a million people to download it, probably just for the lulz, and claim they went platinum in a week. In this day and age anything that goes platinum in its first week is likely to be the only album that year to achieve such a feat. When Lady Gaga did it back in 2011, it was the first time anyone had done it in a good four years.

It might still be worth it to charge a tiny nominal fee, or to give away a shedload of copies of your album for free, if you don't give a rat's ass about the Billboard 200. Which you shouldn't. In an age when the MFN Decemberists can debut at #1, who gives a shit? I don't really count that as an accomplishment anymore. In fact, I'd go so far as to say that if you're on a major label and you can't top the Billboard 200 in 2014, you need to reconsider your career as a recording artist. Really, you shouldn't have a deal anyway. No disrespect to the Decemberists, whom I fuxwit, heavy.

Jay-Z famously gave away a million copies of the dreadfully awful Magna Carta Holy Grail, thus making it a platinum album the day it was released, though I heard that not even a million people actually downloaded it via the Magna Carta Holy Grail app on Samsung Galaxy smartphones. They literally couldn't give a million copies of it away. Maybe some people still illegally downloaded it, either to avoid giving Jay-Z and the Illuminati access to their personal information or because the only phone they could get is from Boost Mobile, due to their credit situation. I guess the RIAA figured a million copies of it were paid for anyway. They could have been rotting in a landfill alongside copies of the ET video game for all they cared. Whereas Billboard changed its rules to keep scammers like Lady Gaga from trying to make it seem as if they went platinum in a week, the RIAA went and changed its rules so that an album didn't have to be out for a month in order to be declared platinum, just so Jay-Z could make it seem like he went platinum in a day, let alone a week.

Rather than releasing 808s & Heartbreak in the fall of '08 and then following it up with a real rap album in the summer of '09, Kanye spent a lot of time getting wasted and engaging in gratuitously inappropriate PDA with Amber Rose, culminating in his performance, if you will, at the '09 VMAs.

Pressure to release a proper follow up to Graduation may have led to his meltdown that year and subsequent media exile, which eventually led to My Beautiful Dark Twisted Fantasy, in 2010.

My Beautiful Dark Twisted Fantasy was originally billed as Kanye's "real hip-hop" album. Pete Rock and the RZA were essentially paid to cosign it, in an attempt to get back in the hip-hop community's good graces.

Kanye loops up the drums from the intro to the song "The Basement" from Mecca and the Soul Brother on "Runaway." As far as I know, that was the extent of Pete Rock's contribution, and I'm at a loss for why he needed to fly out to Hawaii to make it, other than that Kanye wanted him there for a photo op.

There were all kinds of people who were either photographed in the studio with Kanye in California or mentioned in press accounts of the makings of My

Beautiful Dark Twisted Fantasy. Madlib supposedly contributed beats for the album. Mos Def was out there.

In a repeat of what supposedly happened with Jay-Z's Black Album, DJ Premier says that he submitted beats for My Beautiful Dark Twisted Fantasy, but Kanye rejected them all. Actually, I seem to recall hearing that DJ Premier submitted a beat for the Black Album, but he didn't get it in in time. The album was already damn near finished, at that point.

But that doesn't make sense, since it says in Jay-Z's book Decoded that the song "PSA (Public Service Announcement)" was recorded at the very last minute, before they sent the album off to be pressed up. If Jay-Z really wanted a DJ Premier song on that album, he could have had one. Let alone the good half a dozen albums he's released since, none of which have Primo beats on them.

He must have a problem with DJ Premier... and in the absence of any other satisfying explanation, I can't rule out the possibility that it has something to do with Primo's obsession with pron. He's said in interviews that he has a huge, Stanley Kubrick-style collection of pron VHS tapes. Back in the early 2000s, there was a rumor going around that DJ Premier was actually in a pron film.

You don't see it mentioned in garbage slideshows and listicles put together by corporate music blogs because the kids who write them have no idea what took place on the Internets pre-2005. And that's the older ones, the guys who were already into their adulthood at that point. The younger ones are learning about everything they write about literally as they type. And yet these fruits cop such an authoritative tone.

I try to point out some of the more glaring factual errors on sites like Pitchfork just because I don't think people appreciate the scam these sites are trying to pull. You wouldn't take medical advice from a doctor whose only qualifications were that he's white and he has Spotify Premium, now would you? You'd be better off letting Jan Hammer or whatever his name is operate on you.

Jay-Z doesn't want to accept any beats from Primo because he doesn't know where Primo's hands were before he picked up that disc to hand it to Jay-Z. Especially now that Jay-Z has that baby; he doesn't want to run that kind of risk. The baby could end up with herpes on its face.

Years later, I checked XVideos on the outside chance that someone had uploaded the infamous DJ Premier pron film. After all, they've uploaded everything else. I didn't find it, but I did find another pron film DJ Premier was in. It was some sort of vérité thing (I know…), in which a guy follows some chicks from a record store, where they meet DJ Premier, to a restaurant where DJ Premier buys them all chicken and waffles. And then they all go back to a filthy-looking no tell motel a/k/a a sleep n fuck and each earn their $500. But DJ Premier can't join them, because he has a DJ gig that night. Gianna Michaels, Alexis Texas, Gianna Lynn and Penny Flame are all in it.

I read in the comments section at XVideos that the guy in it – the male lead – is in jail on a rape charge. I checked just now, only for the purpose of researching this book, in part to prove that this really did happen, that I'm not just imagining it, and I see that it's long since been removed. So you'll just have to take my word that it exists.

"Power," the lead single from My Beautiful Dark Twisted Fantasy, just ended up sounding like paint by numbers Kanye, not unlike anything that could have appeared on the first few Kanye albums. Nothing about it suggested the more authentic hip-hop sound you might have expected from an album to which Pete Rock, the RZA et al. had been invited to contribute.

It makes sense that he'd want his lead single to have a more commercial sound. However, I don't think you get to make concessions to the marketplace on the one hand, and then co-opt various real hip-hop signifiers on the other hand, probably just in a cynical attempt to essentially buy some street cred.

Eminem pulled something similar around the same time, signing boring-ass Slaughterhouse to Shady Records while bringing in the likes of Pink and Rihanna to sing on his album and recording ballads about drug rehabilitation and spousal abuse. Like the Suit half of Nelly's Sweat/Suit two disc set, Recovery really resonated with rednecks, and probably sold way more copies than it would have otherwise as a result.

Rednecks can relate to songs about drug rehabilitation because many of them are on meth, especially here in my and Eminem's native Midwest. Similarly, as depicted on many an episode of COPS, rednecks live to discipline their women. Their women won't admit to the police that they've been hit, because they understand that getting hit is an integral part of redneck culture. It's not like he meant it.

I wouldn't be surprised if someone in the marketing department at Interscope put Eminem up to recording some of those songs. I know Nelly, now that his rap career is over, has been dominating redneck radio and setting Billboard records with some country song he's got out. Going country is a good career move for older artists who have lost the plot, because people who listen to country could care less whether the music is any good.

"Hootie" from Hootie and the Blowfish, who's not a rapper (though he is black), has also been making major moves out in the sticks. Black people have never been as dominant in country as we are now. It's just that no one gives a shit, because that's the thing that any group of people should aspire to the least. In a sense, it's the exact opposite of when Obama was elected president back in '08.

If Jesse Jackson shed a single tear, it was only because he was reminded of his chronic infidelity.

10
I'mma Let You Finish (Nullus)

If there's one thing white people don't appreciate, it's when a black artist can't show up on time for a concert. Somewhere, there's an aging baby boomer still pissed at Sly Stone for not showing up on time for a concert back in 1975. Never mind the fact that Sly and the Family Stone was an integrated band. We all know it was Sly's fault they couldn't show up on time. Those white guys probably got there early.

Kanye West "ruined" Bonnaroo '08 by showing up two and a half hours late for his set, supposedly because that's how long it took to set up the lights and laser show from his Glow in the Dark tour, which must have looked like a gayer version of the movie Tron, without the bicycles. He wanted the crowd to have the full experience.

I also heard complaints that the show wasn't any good once it finally went on, possibly due to the fact that this was more of a rock crowd, and a jam band crowd at that, which expects real musicianship, not some rapper pacing the stage, grabbing his nuts and shouting expletives – including the dreaded n-word, which is wildly inappropriate for Bonnaroo – to a prerecorded backing track.

Plus, I don't think a laser show was really in keeping with the vibe at Bonnaroo. What's the point of delaying the show for two and a half hours for something a jam band crowd could give a rat's ass about?

———

Earlier that year, there was a minor controversy having to do with the fact that Jay-Z had been selected to headline the Glastonbury Festival, somewhere in Europe. (I only know where the continent is located, not the individual countries. #Murica)

This was viewed, on the Internets, as racist, and it might have been, kinda, but the thing is, live hip-hop often does suck balls. I like rap music, but given a choice, I'd rather go to a rock concert than a rap concert. Certainly, I wouldn't want to go to a festival that was headlined by a rapper. Put the rapper on early, in case he's not any good, and let a rock group headline.

The official explanation was that Glastonbury is typically headlined by guitar bands. It's a guitar band festival. Fans would have been just as pissed if some white EDM act had been scheduled to headlined. Maybe even more so, because EDM is gay.

This all culminated in a stunt in which Jay-Z took to the stage with a guitar around his neck and began his set by singing a few lines from "Wonderwall" by Oasis. One of the guys from Oasis, probably the older, angry one who writes all the songs, was one of the main people complaining about Jay-Z having been selected as headliner.

Video of Jay-Z singing "Wonderwall" was greeted by the hip-hop Internets as one of the greatest civil rights victories since Brown vs. the Board of Education, but then so is pretty much everything Jay-Z ever does. The incident was later referred to in "Jockin' Jay-Z," one of the songs Kanye produced for the Blueprint 3 that wasn't quite good enough to make the cut.

"That bloke from Oasis said I couldn't play guitar," sang Jay-Z. "Somebody should have told him I'm a fuckin' rock star." It's a retarded line, because obviously the bit about him being a rock star is yet another tired reference to his supposed drug dealing past, which doesn't have anything to do with his ability to headline a music festival – unless it's a music festival being put on by FEDS magazine, and I don't know if I'd want to attend a music festival put on by FEDS magazine. It might bring out "the wrong element."

Later that summer, I saw Kanye play Lollapalooza, in Chicago. I imagine his set there was similar to the one he played at Bonnaroo, but minus a lot of the spectacle. No projections of gay guys riding around on glow in the dark motorcycles, thank God.

Whereas Bonnaroo is run by stoned hillbillies, Lollapalooza is easily the most corporate of the summer music festivals, and they weren't about to run the risk of going past their extra-early curfew just because Kanye couldn't figure out how to plug in his computer. They run a tight ship. It's not uncommon to hear a band on the opposite stage start playing over the band who had been playing, if they go over by even a few minutes.

Kanye was one of five headliners that year, along with Radiohead, Wilco, Rage Against the Machine and Nine Inch Nails. One rapper from the 2000s and four '90s-era rock bands. Kanye was playing opposite Nine Inch Nails. I guess the idea was counterprogramming, like when they schedule a romantic comedy to be released the same weekend as a big action movie, for girls. They had Wilco playing opposite Rage Against the Machine, whom I'd seen the year before at Rock the Bells in New York.

At the time, Kanye was easily the biggest artist of the bunch in terms of record sales, radio spins and what have you, but if he'd been selected as headliner of the entire festival, which was Radiohead, people would have been pissed. The festival might not have sold out.

Later, I saw Atmosphere play the same stage Kanye played, and they drew a much larger crowd – and that was in the middle of the afternoon. The night Kanye headlined, most people must have either gone to catch Nine Inch Nails or taken off early. Maybe they heard about his set at Bonnaroo and were like, "Fuck that shit!"

I planned to catch Nine Inch Nails, but I ended up creepily following some chick I met earlier that day to see Kanye. She was there with some people who wanted to see Nine Inch Nails, but she wanted to see Kanye (again, counterprogramming), so she was left alone, which is one of the things I look for in a woman. She was like, Are you going to see Kanye? And I was like, Of course I'm going to see Kanye!

Shit, it could have been Nickelback. #priorities

This was at a performance by a group named Plastic Little. How they got to play Lollapalooza I have no idea. Pharrell must have pulled some strings. Seemingly no one in the crowd had any idea who they were. This chick asked a few other people, and they didn't know. She asked me, and I told her who it was. I know the names of a lot of obscure rap groups, from having written about rap music on the Internets for over 10 years now. My email inbox is a goddamn tragedy.

Plastic Little ended up having a second minor brush with fame a good half a decade later, in 2013, when one of their songs was sampled in that song "Harlem Shake" by Baauer. The part where the guy says, "Then do the Harlem Shake." Wub wub wub.

"Harlem Shake" became a huge Internets meme, generating hundreds of millions of views on YouTube. In these videos, people would just be sitting around not doing anything, and then when the guy says Harlem Shake they'd start jumping around and dancing. There was one where Tess Ellen took her shirt off. That may have been my favorite. Last I checked, it was still on the Internets. But not on YouTube. You gotta go to a site called Dailymotion.

The way the Billboard Hot 100 is tabulated was changed to include YouTube views, and "Harlem Shake" immediately shot to #1. Diplo's label Mad Decent, which originally released the song as a free Internets download in 2012, hired one of those companies that troll YouTube looking for unauthorized uses of a song, but rather than filing a copyright infringement claim with YouTube and having the video removed, they run ads alongside it, the proceeds of which are split between YouTube, i.e. Google, the copyright troll firm and the artist. Those ads pay, on average, about $9 for every 1,000 views, which is Jack Schitt on a per view basis, but keep in mind how many times those Harlem Shake videos were viewed back in 2013. Diplo, Baauer et al. probably made a mint.

I never go to these festivals with the intention of meeting women, but I have on several occasions, which leads me to believe that if you went with the specific purpose of trying to bang chicks you could clean up – or at least score, which is cleaning up for me personally.

One time, a chick did randomly start making out with me during a set by the Hold Steady. Handsome as I am, I think she was overcome by the power of the music, which really is that good. Or she may have just been the kind of slut who enjoys making out with random guys at parties, and of all the guys there, she figured I was least likely to object, which of course I didn't. She was free to use my body as her personal plaything.

Some people were supposedly getting it on during Rage Against the Machine's set, the same year Kanye was at Lollapalooza. I wasn't close enough to get a look, which has been one of my life's great disappointments. The next day, Perry Farrell, who gives off a real creep vibe, mentioned it during his set with a (once again) reunited Jane's Addiction.

Jane says, beat this pussy up right out in the open.

Also, come to think of it, some people got it on in a porta potty at Rock the Bells the year before – which is disgusting. Probably some tweakers. I don't know if I'd want to have sex with a girl who would have sex in a porta potty at Rock the Bells. Which is not to say that I definitely wouldn't.

My logistics usually aren't right for bringing a chick home to make sweet, passionate love, staying at the Y, sleeping in a room with several other guys (with one eye open, natch). I haven't had enough money to go to festivals on the reg since 2010, and even when I did I couldn't afford such luxuries as a hotel room. I went to the Pitchfork Music Festival in 2012, a few days after my first book came out, but only because my parents bought me a ticket. Yeah, I was 31 years old at the time. What of it?

If enough people buy this book, I'll be returning to Lollapalooza 2015 on a proverbial white horse. If I make like a million dollars from it, I really will show up on a white horse, promise. If it's only kinda successful, maybe I'll show up high on cocaine. Don't tell the police though. Lord knows I've got enough problems. (If El-P's there, I'll "borrow" some from El-P.)

The white backlash against Kanye, which dates back to the Hurricane Katrina telethon and which picked up steam when Kanye "ruined" Bonnaroo, kicked into high gear with the Taylor Swift incident at the '09 VMAs.

It actually worked out well for MTV, because it created a buzz around the VMAs which hadn't been there since the late '90s. Ratings for the VMAs hadn't been right ever since Sunday night became the night to watch great TV dramas on networks like HBO and AMC.

The night of the '09 VMAs was the same night as the season finale of True Blood and a great episode of Mad Men. I watched those two and DVRd the VMAs, but I never did end up watching the VMAs, because all of the best parts were excerpted for my viewing pleasure on the Internets, like a Lord of Cumshots compilation on Xvideos.

MTV probably doesn't make as much, or maybe not anything at all, if you DVR a show and watch bits and pieces of it the next day, or just catch the highlights of it on the Internets. That's why it was so difficult to find video of Kanye bumrushing Taylor Swift's acceptance speech. If they couldn't get anyone to watch it live, at the very least they wanted to wrap the video in their janky, proprietary online video player, which bombards you with ads and probably somehow steals your personal information and sells it to credit card companies.

They probably don't make shit from those online videos compared to what they'd make if you'd watch it live, but then it's not like they have any choice in the matter. They're desperate. If they're only gonna make $0.10, they still need that $0.10. Manhattan real estate is pricey. They might have to move MTV from Times Square to the building BET is in and move BET to somewhere in the Bronx – which of course would be billed as a return to the birthplace of hip-hop.

The night's big draw was supposed to be Lady Gaga. A press release had gone out announcing that her performance would be the modern day equivalent of Madonna's performance at the '84 VMAs. I was only three years old during the '84 VMAs (so was MTV), so I only recall seeing Madonna's performance years after the fact. I can only imagine what it would have been like to have been, say, 28, the age I was during the '09 VMAs.

My parents weren't even 28 back then. My parents are about the same age as Madonna. My mom seemed older than Madonna then, but now she seems to be a good decade younger than Madonna. It's true what they say: Black don't crack. Also, as KRS-One predicted, Madonna has taken to calling her son the dreaded n-word on Instagram. What goes around comes around, I figure.

There was a rumor going around that Lady Gaga is not really a girl, in the sense that she was born with a peen, or some sort of weird hybrid genitalia, like a ginormous clit. A clit, from what I understand (I didn't take health class in high school), is essentially a tiny peen on a woman, similar to how men have nipples for no apparent reason. That's one of the reasons why you shouldn't suck on it. Especially if it's bigger than average.

In several pictures of Lady Gaga that hit the Internets that year it does in fact look like she has a ginormous clit. It's too small to be a peen (nullus), but it's not like any camel toe I've ever seen – and I've seen my share.

It could be that she tried to pierce it herself, and it got infected, like how you'll sometimes see a skanky scene girl walking around with a nasty keloid dangling from her ear. On the one hand, it's gross-looking, but on the other hand, it's one of the more certain guarantees of sexual promiscuity. It's actually one of the things I look for in a woman. A crotch keloid, though? She'd have to have a pretty impressive pair of cans.

There was also a rumor going around that one of the girls in Beyoncé's "Single Ladies" video was a tranny. I had yet to see the "Single Ladies" video when the incident at the VMAs happened. I thought about watching both it and the Taylor Swift video, to see which one is better, but then it occurred to me: What if that rumor is true? Plus, I didn't really want to see either of those videos anyway. Who gives a shit which one is better. Well, aside from Kanye.

Having never seen either of them, I still feel pretty confident in saying that neither of them is amongst the best music videos of all time, of ALL TIME. The best music video of all time is "Losing My Religion" by REM, which was directed by an Indian guy named Tarsem. He later directed a movie called The Cell starring Jennifer Lopez. It's either terrible or mind-blowingly brilliant, depending on whom you ask. It got mediocre reviews when it came out, and Jennifer Lopez is in it, but David Fincher and Spike Jonze supposedly swear by it.

Response to the Taylor Swift incident on the Internets was as harsh as it was immediate.

World Star had a video of a fat Mexican kid calling Kanye the dreaded n-word. You'd think Kanye had snatched the microphone from Selena Gomez, not Taylor Swift. Mexican kids must fuxwit Taylor Swift heavy. I know a lot of them are really into Morrissey, as discussed in Chuck Klosterman IV, and they refuse to believe he's gay.

It's difficult for us regular Muricans to imagine what it must be like to see a girl who's taller than every guy in your entire country, but in a way that's still feminine and adorable. Because she's on the thin side and she has a somewhat unique face, Taylor Swift might honestly be the single most underrated beauty of our time. Very few guys on the Internets will admit to being sexually attracted to her (as if), but I bet she has an amazing physical presence, if you were to see her in person.

Not that she needs me defending her. She's probably got over a hundred million dollars already, and she's barely in her 20s. All I've got is this buskit. Fuck Taylor Swift! I will say that, given a choice, I'd much rather listen to Taylor Swift than Beyoncé. Beyoncé's music is terrible.

Beyoncé invented (or at least popularized) the terrible style of singing everyone does on American Idol, where you draw out each syllable and really put some stank on it, to prove how well you can sing. She's like a professional version of the ex-crackhead who gets up and does an a capella version of Mariah Carey's "Hero" during the banquet portion of a family reunion. Why is that even a career? Not that I actually want to listen to Taylor Swift. I'm not Tom Breihan. I'm just making a point here.

Someone actually sent me the petition I'd created five years prior to have Kanye West banned from the Grammys. It must still be floating around the Internets somewhere. If you come across it, I wouldn't sign it, if I were you. That site struck me as sketchy even back then, and what difference does it make at this point anyway?

It only ever got about 500 signatures back in '04, but by the time of the Taylor Swift incident it was up to over 2,000. There was a place where you could leave a brief comment alongside your name, and I noticed that a lot of people had left angry comments about what he did to Taylor Swift at the VMAs. They didn't want to see a repeat of this at the Grammys. And generally speaking, I don't think they wanted his career to continue on after that point.

Bossip, one of our finer black websites, went through and screencapped where a lot of white people on Twitter were calling Kanye the dreaded n-word. Using a few simple search strings, you can put together a similar post any time black people are in the news, even now that a lot of people have been fired from their jobs for things they've said on Twitter. You gotta have a job in the first place in order to get fired. And this is 2014, not 1994. Shit, I'm about to go on Twitter and say something inappropriate as soon as I get done working on this. #MidasWhale

---

There was a lot of racial tension on Twitter in the summer of '09, leading up to the Taylor Swift incident, because that was around the time when black people found the site and proceeded to pretty much ruin it. Or fix it, depending on how you look at it.

You wouldn't notice it during the day, if you didn't follow any hoodrats. Twitter was the same as it always had been. But you'd notice, first thing in the morning, there'd be some decidedly ratchet trending topics left over from the night before, e.g. #uainthittinitright

If she can still fix her mouth to tell you to stop... #uainthittinitright

The '09 BET Awards may have been the first time the trending topics were dominated by hoodrat fare during waking hours. The names of several celebs were trending, but these weren't celebs in the traditional sense of the term, meaning someone most people would recognize. Some of them were names that most white people wouldn't recognize, leading to concern that Twitter may have been on the fritz.

The only white person whose name was trending was OxyClean pitchman Billy Mays, who'd died that day, and it's hard to knock someone from the trending topics the day they died. He was found dead in his home, and it was announced that he'd been hit in the head by a piece of carry-on luggage that had shifted its position in the bin mid-flight, probably because it hadn't been properly secured. (Who wants to bet it belonged to a woman?)

Later it was revealed that he'd probably just OD'd on coke. In retrospect, it doesn't seem at all surprising that a guy from a TV informercial would be on coke. How else can you get that excited about Simoniz? That luggage story never did sit quite right with me, though about two years later to the day I lost my right eye in a similar accident. A cardboard box almost killed me. God spared my life because he wanted me to write this book.

It's true what they say. The lord does work in mysterious ways.

How else to explain the fact that these things all seem to be related? Billy Mays died three days after Michael Jackson, and he was almost the exact same age as Michael Jackson. Billy Mays was the only white person trending during the BET Awards, where there was a tribute to Michael Jackson. Billy Mays was a cracka-ass cracka. Michael Jackson bleached his skin. Billy Mays' luxurious beard was almost certainly the result of grecian formula. Michael Jackson had a detachable nose. They both probably died from drugs.

For all intents and purposes ("intensive purposes"), the '09 BET Awards was the beginning of Black People Twitter. I began blogging about Black People Twitter back in '09. Hoodrats themselves discovered Black People Twitter in 2013. An article by Buzzfeed's black employee was commissioned, which caused the floors to go unswept for a period of time. Someone created a Black Twitter Wikipedia entry. One hoodrat even announced that she was writing a book about Black Twitter. It made me feel that much better about having written Infinite Crab Meats, which, incidentally, discusses Black People Twitter.

2013 was a big year for "discoveries" on the Internets. Later that year, it was discovered that R. Kelly peed on a girl on video back in the late '90s. And then 2014 kicked off with the revelation that Woody Allen is married to (not really) his stepdaughter and that he was accused of diddling his adopted daughter back in 1992. I fear for Matthew Broderick. It's only a matter of time before people find out that he once killed 11 people in Ireland, for which he was fined $70, let alone the fact that he was banging the chick who played his sister in Ferris Bueller's Day Off. Is my childhood not sacred?

There was some speculation that the Taylor Swift incident was staged.

The '09 VMAs ended up being the highest-rated VMAs since 2002. I'm not sure if that was from the initial broadcast or if was also counting reruns, after Kanye snatching the mic from Taylor Swift was all over the news. Regardless, you had to know MTV would try to spin it as a huge ratings success and evidence of the VMAs' enduring relevancy.

A few people pointed out that the camera angles seemed a little bit too perfect, though you'd expect them to be, since this took place right there at the podium. If they had the camera trained squarely on Taylor Swift, it wouldn't have been too difficult to zoom out some, to also capture Kanye. The people who operate those cameras are trained professionals, I would imagine. But why wasn't anything done to stop Kanye? Someone could have tackled him before he even go to the stage, and MTV could have easily cut away or gone to commercial once he launched into his little spiel.

I read on Drunken Stepfather that Kanye West and Taylor Swift have the same agent. Jesus from Drunken Stepfather would know some shit like that, because he's plugged into the Hollywood scene. He's one of the most well-connected people I know. The only reason I wouldn't list him as a reference if I was trying to get a job in an elementary school is because his site is positively filthy. TMZ used to post links to his posts in their sidebar, until a Hollywood exec spotted a post he did on how Paul Walker was a sex offender, a few days after the actor died in a fiery crash.

Comedy equals tragedy plus time. If it bends, it's funny. If it breaks, it's not funny! (c) Alan Alda

Earlier that year, there was a fake incident during the MTV Movie Awards. To promote Bruno, the gay version of Borat, Sasha Baron Cohen descended from the ceiling on a wire, landing on Eminem upside down with his legs straddling Eminem's face and his balls hanging out of his shorts, getting all kinds of fromunda cheese on Eminem's lips.

Eminem, who must have been mic'd up, sounded pissed. He'd been accused of being homophobic 10 years before, so it made sense that he'd be upset to have another guy's balls in his face, but he didn't commit a hate crime or anything. He didn't even shove Sasha Baron Cohen's balls away from his face.

It later came out that this was almost certainly staged. Cohen obviously had the Bruno film coming out. Eminem's Relapse had been released about two weeks before. The old Eminem would have put a shoe on Sasha Baron Cohen and called him a fag in the process. The circa '09 Eminem couldn't even be bothered to take shots at Asher Roth, who tried to bogart the promo cycle for Relapse with that "I Love College" song he had out and sorta kinda dissed Eminem in an interview. Used to be, you couldn't even say anything nice about Eminem in an interview without incurring his wrath.

A few weeks later, video emerged of Mos Def at a show in Baltimore. Introducing a song, he announced that it was produced by Kanye West. The crowd erupted in a chorus of boos. It wasn't clear if they were pissed at Kanye because of the Taylor Swift thing or because they were salty backpackers. Kanye had once been something of a backpacker himself, the self-proclaimed only dreaded n-word with a Benz and a backpack. Back when he was still trying to put together a following.

Mos Def was like (and I'm paraphrasing), "Hold on a sec! It's not like he slapped the bitch. All he did was voice an opinion that you were at home agreeing with. It may not have been at the most appropriate time, but it's not like he didn't apologize."

He went on to compare the outrage over the VMAs incident to the lack of outrage over South Carolina Congressman Joe Wilson calling Obama a liar during the State of the Union address, while he was trying to talk, and a redneck preacher who delivered a sermon in which he threatened to kill the president.

I thought he brought up a good point about the absurdity of hip-hop heads being pissed at a rapper for bumrushing a pop singer. That's what hip-hop is supposed to be all about, right? KRS-One (really, one of his weed carriers) once threw PM Dawn from a stage. Mos Def once pulled up outside the MTV Awards on a flatbed truck from which he dissed Bono, of all people, and performed a song about Hurricane Katrina.

Kanye apologized to Taylor Swift three times – twice on his blog, and then over the phone. Four times, really, if you count the part where he said that he was happy for her and that he'd let her finish as an apology.

The mistake he made – well, one of the mistakes he made – was falling into the trap of trying to apologize to someone over the Internets. You should never apologize to someone who's called for you to apologize to them via the media anyway, because it's a trick.

Only thing that's gonna happen is, they're gonna say it wasn't a good enough apology, and you'll either be forced to apologize again, or refuse to apologize again, which is worse than not having apologized in the first place.

Who ever heard of analyzing someone's apology to decide whether or not it's good enough? What kind of bullshit is that? If you sense that someone might pull some shit like that, I wouldn't apologize to them in the first place, even if you really were in the wrong. Fuck 'em!

At the very least, I'd consult the Google to see if they've demanded an apology before and how it turned out. The fact that they would even demand an apology (as if) is a red flag, really, unless it's for something they had to be hospitalized for. It suggests to me that they aren't a serious person.

You'd think rappers would have learned, after seeing what happened to Kanye, but no. Four years later, after some woman took objection to Rawse's date rape anthem "U.O.E.N.O," Rawse caved and issued an apology. Several of them, in fact.

First he went on the radio and made it clear that he doesn't personally condone date rape, just because he wrote a song about it. (So did A Tribe Called Quest!) Then he went on Twitter and actually apologized. He reiterated that he's officially against rape, that's not what "U.O.E.N.O" is about, and he's sorry if that's what you took from it. He also apologized to Reebok, his sponsor, for any inconvenience this may have caused them.

The feminist group who was protesting his deal with Reebok refused to accept his apology. If only there was a way he could have forced it on them. They didn't say what exactly they wanted him to do, they just said what he did wasn't good enough. Women...

Reebok supposedly dropped Rawse from his endorsement deal with them, and it was only then that he issued an official statement. The feminist group didn't bother responding one way or the other, because they'd already gotten what they came for, which was to threaten a black man's livelihood. They were too busy celebrating.

The whole getting dropped by Reebok and issuing a statement thing was probably just a charade anyway, like Eminem and Sasha Baron Cohen at the MTV Movie Awards, or (maybe) Kanye West and Taylor Swift at the VMAs. Later that summer Rawse was back doing commercials for them.

If Reebok really did fake dropping Rawse just to get that feminist group to go harass someone else, you have to respect that, regardless of where you stand on the issues. They took it to a new level of warfare. They went straight Sun Tzu on those whiny bitches. Imagine if South Africa had pulled the same shit on Nelson Mandela. According to Naomi Klein's The Shock Doctrine, they kinda did. That may have been the origin of Reebok's strategy for dealing with feminist groups.

Kanye was supposed to go out on tour with Lady Gaga that fall, which ended up being canceled. First I heard that a few dates were canceled, probably because tickets went on sale and hardly anyone bought them, either due to backlash from the VMAs incident or general lack of interest. No one really cared for the tour he went on behind Graduation, when he "ruined" Bonnaroo and mostly went ignored at Lollapalooza.

Sometimes they use the VMAs to kick off a fall tour by the big corporate acts du jour. Perhaps the most famous example of this, and my favorite example anyway, was when Courtney Love and Marilyn Manson performed at the '98 VMAs, when I was a senior in high school, and then tried to go out on tour. That lasted for all of about two dates before it ground to a screeching halt due to bickering between the two headliners and, I would imagine, drugs.

Later the guy from New Radicals, the white Kanye in a sense, dissed both Courtney Love and Marilyn Manson, along with Beck and Hanson, on "You Get What You Give," one of the best songs of all time, of ALL TIME. Asked about it in an interview, Marilyn Manson said that he was most upset about being mentioned in the same sentence as Courtney Love, and that he'd crack the guy from New Radicals' skull open. Marilyn Manson gave a lot of astute interviews, especially after Columbine, which happened right around that same time.

A few weeks later it was announced that Lady Gaga was going out on tour again, this time by herself, and she was doing brisk business in ticket sales.

The kind of white girls who were going to see Lady Gaga probably didn't have much interest in Kanye West in the first place, and now they were pissed at him for what he did to Taylor Swift. They were probably willing to pay the same price just to see Lady Gaga by herself. White girls and Kanye West are never, ever getting back together.

Before, it was definitely a matter of Lady Gaga taking Kanye West out on a tour with her and not vice versa. Rappers have to team up with a few garbage R&B groups or a white pop artist in order to play stadiums.

There just isn't sufficient interest in rap music to fill a stadium, unless you bring eight artists and have them each play a 15 minute set, which is just retarded. The last time I saw a big package rap tour (nullus) was Hard Knock Life, back in maybe '99, when I was a senior in high school, near the commercial zenith of Def Jam-style commercial rap.

Even if they could find enough people willing to pay to see someone grabbing his crotch, pacing the stage and shouting obscenities to a pre-recorded backing track, it probably costs more to insure if it's a full-on rap show.

Now if you see Jay-Z go out on tour, it's Jay-Z and Justin Timberlake, or before that, Jay-Z and Beyoncé. Who amongst those of us who had Reasonable Doubt the week it came out (and I realize this is literally no one on the 2014 hip-hop Internets) is interested in seeing a set by Justin Timberlake or Beyoncé? Kanye tried to go on tour with just Kendrick "Hobbit Hands" Lamar and ended up playing to half empty stadiums – though that was due in part to the fact that Hobbit Hands is an overrated industry hype.

11

One Less Lonely Dreaded N-Word

One of the first casualties of this declining interest in Kanye West was Pastelle, the clothing line he'd been threatening to release since back in '05. It was finally announced that Pastelle had been shuttered once and for all in the fall of '09. If the Taylor Swift incident a few weeks before wasn't the impetus for the TIs pulling the plug, it definitely didn't help matters.

Pastelle probably wouldn't have sold anyway. The rapper clothing line bubble had already burst, at that point. Remember when Outkast had their own clothing line? That might not have hit department stores. It might have gone straight to Marshall's, TJ Maxx, Ross for Less and what have you.

Plus, not very many guys are gonna wear clothes made by a company called Pastelle. That doesn't sound sufficiently masculine. Not too long after Pastelle was dropped like a bad habit, Kanye started performing in a skirt. Is that what Pastelle was supposed to be?

St. Louis' own Nelly had a clothing line called Vokal that I never saw anyone wearing, but you still see the occasional hoodrat wearing a pair of Apple Bottoms jeans, to this day. That's because it's the only clothing line designed specifically for women with ginormous asses, if you don't count Ashley Stewart.

Apple Bottoms was destined to lose out to Ashley Stewart in the long run, because many Ashley Stewart stores are conveniently located in strip malls in marginal areas, sandwiched in between a Chinese restaurant and a Korean-owned beauty supply. It's the definition of one-stop shopping, for a certain kind of woman. If there's a check-cashing place down on the corner, you don't even have to stop somewhere else to get cash. I try to avoid strip malls like that at all costs, on the 1st and 15th, delicious though Chinese food may be.

Ecko, which had been the uniform for rednecks and wiggers throughout the 2000s (it's since been supplanted by South Pole, since you can't find Ecko in as many places anymore), had either already been sold off to the Chinese for pennies on the dollar or would be very soon.

I remember reading in the paper that they borrowed a shedload of money to build fancy offices with a basketball court in them. Think about how much money it must cost to build an office large enough to house a basketball court in Manhattan. Enough, I guess, to cost them a clothing line that must have been making them money hand over fist throughout the 2000s. They'd probably still be making a shedload of money from it today.

People out in the flyover states still wear hip-hop clothes. And not just dumbass kids. You see senior citizens, retarded people who live in a facility... pretty much anyone who rides on a Sunset Coach wearing it, because you can find so much of that shit at discount retailers for less than you'd think it would cost to make – except when you consider that it was almost certainly made in a sweatshop. Extremely fat people wear it because hip-hop clothes are so big.

Ecko comes in sizes up to umpteenx, big enough for a sumo wrestler to wear (but probably too long), and even the regular sizes are bigger than they should be. A 2x in a hip-hop shirt is the same size as a 4x in a regular shirt. You end up looking like an idiot, even if – like me – you believe that a man's clothes should be at least kinda loose-fitting. God intended for your nuts to be able to breathe. That's why he put them in a separate bag on the outside of your body. Don't question Allah's infinite wisdom.

I don't think Complex got to keep that office with the basketball court in it either. A building they were in recently was the building mentally unstable hipster rapper Capital Steez leaped to his death from. He was able to get in at night and go up to the roof because his manager or somebody had office space there.

They were involved in some sort of scam with Marc Ecko in which Ecko was both promoting Joey Bada$$ and his Pro Era group of weed carriers and also running a magazine that was reporting on them. Bada$$ was given a fake executive position with Ecko not unlike Alicia Keys' position with Blackberry.

When Alicia Keys became an exec with Blackberry, she famously announced it in a tweet that was sent from an iPhone. She's since been fired.

Joey Bada$$ makes '90s-style throwback rap, and his videos look like b-roll footage from that movie The Wackness, minus the adorable Olivia Thirlby. Marc Ecko was probably hoping this would lead to a return of '90s-style hip-hop clothes. I don't know if he has a stake in Ecko clothes anymore, now that it's owned by the Chinese, but he could probably put together something else along those lines, if that's not a condition of his deal with the Chinese.

Alas, it doesn't seem like Joey Bada$$ will be able to get much traction. A$AP Rocky, who dresses like a fruit, started out doing knockoff versions of southern rap, but since he (sorta kinda) blew up, he's done songs where he's ripped off Joey Bada$$' steez wholesale and seemed to have more success with it. It could be that Joey Bada$$ is just too ugly a kid. A$AP Rocky, at a glance, almost looks like a chick, albeit a "dark butt." He wouldn't last 15 minutes in prison.

Kanye, for his part, insists that the Taylor Swift incident was to blame for Pastelle's downfall, almost seeming to suggest one day on Twitter that the fashion execs he was dealing with really were interested in what Swift's acceptance speech would have been. And now they'll never know.

That may have been a bit of a stretch, but I definitely wouldn't rule out a white backlash as a contributing factor. Interest in his music hasn't been the same ever since, and it stands to reason that interest in any ancillary products would follow suit; CACs wouldn't be any more interested in buying one of Kanye's pink polo shirts than they'd be in buying a set of OJ Simpson-brand golf clubs. Granted, what OJ did was somewhat worse than what Kanye did. The same logic still applies. These things don't come down to a matter of degree. Once white people are done with you, that's it. Ask some of my old managers in fast food.

But there's still the matter of whether or not anyone would have bought Pastelle even before Kanye ran afoul of the white community. Lest we forget, this brand had been gestating for something like half a decade at that point. Kanye's image probably wasn't the only thing wrong with it, and backlash from the Taylor Swift incident may have just been a convenient excuse for his financial backers to cut their losses.

The time to drop a line of hip-hop clothes was back in the late '90s, or maybe the early 2000s at the latest. When Jay-Z sold off however much of Rocafella he actually owned to the same company that makes half the shit you see at Target, back in the late '00s, it was just in time. I haven't seen anyone who isn't either old, retarded or morbidly obese in Rocawear ever since.

Kanye famously refused to join Twitter for the first few years. He once posted a rant about it on his fake blog/scam travel site. You could tell it was really him posting, because the text was in ALL CAPS and the grammar was all fucked the fuck up.

It wasn't always him posting. In an interview, New York magazine asked about his blogging process. He responded that he has a couple of kids who work for him. If he sees something interesting, he'll call and tell them to do a post on it. Before, he'd been caught copying and pasting content from other sites, including New York magazine, without attribution, essentially passing off other people's work as his own.

He didn't see anything wrong with passing off other people's work as his own, because he had other people writing his rhymes from jump, and eventually he had other people making beats for him. Even before, his production technique consisted of wanton sampling.

Also, he might be self-conscious about not being able to effectively convey his thoughts via the written word. He might even be functionally illiterate. Some of the rants he's obviously typed himself, in ALL CAPS, don't make any more sense than, say, his comments at the Katrina telethon, i.e. the stuff leading up to the part about how George Bush doesn't care about black people.

The Internets long suspected that it wasn't really Kanye writing most of the posts. This was confirmed when he somehow managed to post while he was locked up for attacking that stalkerazzi. He'd failed to come up with a system in which, if he were detained for some reason, his ghostwriters would hold off on posting until he gave them the all clear.

Something similar once happened with conservative blogger Michelle Malkin, who got caught updating her blog at times when she couldn't possibly have been able to post. It was suspected that her husband was writing her posts for her. She was the same one who suggested that Hurricane Katrina looters, i.e. any black people who went looking for food after the storm hit, should be shot on sight.

There was once a fake Kanye West Twitter account that had over a million followers. This was back before Twitter cracked down on people making fake accounts for celebrities. There's still plenty of fake celeb accounts, but now you can't make a fake celeb account with the actual name of the celeb. If it's a parody Kanye West account, for example, it has to be called Not Kanye West, or something to that effect, and it probably has to clearly state in the bio that it's a fake/parody account.

Using someone else's name and likeness to attract followers on Twitter is still one of the wealth strategies I recommend for Generation Y, along with, for the ladies, uploading gratuitous photos of your ass in yoga pants and trying to get guys to either buy you things from an Amazon wishlist, or pay you just to respond to emails, via a site called MyGirlFund (I get deep into this kind of career move in my second book, Infinite Crab Meats), and uploading someone else's intellectual property to YouTube and running Google AdSense alongside it.

YouTube is notorious for not bothering to enforce copyright law, except if they can somehow make money from it. If it's a situation like the song "Harlem Shake" by Baauer, where a company can go through, find every single Harlem Shake video that was ever uploaded to the Internets (except for the Tess Ellen one), and collect on any ad revenue that it generates, even though Baauer, Diplo et al. didn't have shit to do with making those videos, then YouTube is all for it. But if it's a situation where the artist is long since dead, or too old to use the Internets, YouTube could give a rat's ass who uploads and then profits from their video.

Similarly, the key to making money shamelessly exploitng someone else's name, likeness, personality and what have you on Twitter is to focus on people who somehow have yet to join. People who suffer from drug addiction, mental illness and rappers who are in jail would all be excellent choices.

For years, there was some guy pretending to be Katt Williams. One day I noticed he was tweeting ads for some shit that would probably destroy your computer if you clicked on it. If you can gather enough followers, you can make pretty good money posting ads. Kim Kardashian is said to make $10,000 per tweet. Not per day, mind you. Per tweet. Shit, years of my life have gone by when I haven't made $10,000. And it wasn't when I was 13 either. Why would I have been working at 13?

Katt Williams has since created his own account, but I checked just now and I see that the guy with the fake account still has the handle @KattWilliams. There's no way a sober person in their right mind wouldn't just have their people call Twitter and put Jack Dorsey on notice. That's why I suggest focusing on celebs with either drug problems, mental illness or both.

"Special Delivery" rapper G-Dep falls into the rare category of celebrity who's both crazy and on drugs, and he's also in jail. If he had much of a following, that would definitely be the best celebrity's identity to hijack. As it is, the fake G-Dep account only ever had about 400 followers. Which is tragic, really, because the fake G-Dep account was the only amusing parody account in the history of Twitter. The hilarious thing about it was that it was written as if it really was G-Dep on Twitter trying to get his career back in order... but it didn't make sense how G-Dep could be on Twitter, when he was probably off wandering through an alley somewhere in Harlem dusted out of his mind on PCP.

There's no indication that G-Dep has ever used the Internets. He's in jail now, and I don't know if they allow inmates to access the Internets, because they might try to look up how to break out of prison on WikiHow. Also, there's a case to be made that the only way people in prison should have computers is if they somehow pay for them themselves.

If G-Dep was at all, ahem, adept at finding information on the Internets, you'd think he would have looked up whether or not the guy he shot back in 1993 was still alive. When he turned himself in for it, in 2011, he said he had no idea whether or not the guy had died. If he couldn't have found a newspaper article or something on it in Google, he probably could have at least found the guy's name in a phone book and called his house pretending to be Publishers Clearing House. If someone picked up and said that the guy had been dead for going on 20 years, then obviously you wouldn't head down to the station and admit to having shot him.

G-Dep says he had to turn himself in because he was haunted by the guilt. That was probably just the PCP talking. Pimp C thought he was being followed too (by a group of leprechauns, and a woman), and he also ended up in jail.

Two years after G-Dep turned himself in, Baauer's "Harlem Shake" became one of the biggest songs of all time. It topped the Billboard Hot 100, in a year when not a single black artist reached that summit, just off of views on YouTube. (The mp3 was a free download.) As aggressively monetized as it was, it probably generated like a billion dollars. If G-Dep could have booked one show from it, he might have made enough to keep himself in angel dust for a couple of years.

Checking the fake G-Dep Twitter just now, I see that it's only been updated twice since late 2010, right around the time Dep turned himself in, once after "Harlem Shake" the song blew TF up and I pointed out how tragic it was that G-Dep wasn't around to capitalize on it, because he stupidly turned himself in for a crime he'd gotten away with for damn near 20 years, and then again about a year later when Kanye's tour DJ, A-Trak, praised his "timing," ironically enough. The kid who runs it, a Ras Kass stan from Canada, must have a Google Alert set for any mentions of G-Dep.

Kanye eventually signed up for Twitter, probably desperate to try to promote My Beautiful Dark Twisted Fantasy. Whereas the fake Kanye West account from the early days of Twitter had over a million followers, the new, real Kanye West account stalled out at about 250,000, far behind some of the top celebs on Twitter, like Justin Bieber a/k/a Biebler, Katy Perry, who, if she ever posted a picture of her cans might break the Internets, and his future baby's mother, all of whom had 10s of millions of followers. It was a sign of the state his career was in.

Kanye's Twitter following has since grown to about 10 million – 10x as many followers as the fake Kanye account ever had, albeit at a time when way more people are on Twitter. He's benefited from numerous stunts and controversies, including the time when he went off on Jimmy Kimmel, suggesting that there's something wrong with Kimmel's face, that he doesn't get any pussy, and that he's not as funny as Sarah Silverman. No disrespect to Ben Affleck. 10 million followers is still only about a fifth as many as Biebler or Katy Perry.

In order to try to boost his social media status ahead of the release of My

Beautiful Dark Twisted Fantasy, he shamelessly trolled Justin Bieber, probably hoping to get a retweet or a Follow Friday. One time he @replied Biebler to point out how amazing it was that Biebler was born in 1994 (almost 13 years to the day after I was born), and that was the year he first got some stank on his hanglow. This, according to Kanye, was an example of the circle of life, as sung about by Elton John in The Lion King, which also came out in 1994. On my blog, I joked that Kanye might be Biebler's father.

At the time, Biebler was often seen in public with Kim Kardashian. It was the equivalent of one of those relationships in which two celebs get together seemingly primarily for the purpose of getting their names in the paper. I figured Biebler probably wasn't hitting that, because he was 16 years old at the time and Kim Kardashian is my age. She was old enough at that point that I'm not sure a 16 year-old would even be interested. I don't know if people in Canada have any concept of a tank ass, let alone an interest in one. A reporter actually asked Kim Kardashian if the two of them were an item. She replied that she enjoyed spending time with him, and if he wasn't a 16 year-old boy she'd definitely let him hit that. It probably wouldn't have hurt if he was black, too. Lil Bow Wow would have scaled that tank ass like Mount Everest.

I consulted a search engine to see what Biebler and Kanye had discussed, aside from Kanye's potential paternity. If you're familiar with search engine operators, which I learned how to use in my sideline collecting hot chicks' selfies, it's pretty easy to dig up conversations on Twitter, even if they've long since been buried underneath a deluge of subsequent tweets, @replies and what have you. Years later, some young guy took advantage of this to dig up all the instances in which rappers had talked shit about people they were ostensibly cool with, especially Wale, whom no one really likes.

Come to find out, Biebler had never replied to one of Kanye's tweets a day in his life. Kanye's relationship with Biebler was just as one-sided as any number of teenage girls' imagined relationships with Biebler. Granted, I'm sure it's difficult to know if any one person in particular tweeted at you, when you've got 50 million followers. If you follow that person, you can set it to where it only shows mentions from people you follow, but Biebler follows a shedload of people too. So that's not gonna work. Imagine if he accidentally set his phone to go off every time someone @replied him. It would literally explode. Those iPhones have been known to randomly catch fire while people are talking on them. It's the 2014 equivalent of a book of matches catching fire in your pocket (but less dangerous to your junk).

Weeks later, when it was announced that Kanye and Raekwon, who'd gone out to Hawaii to work on My Beautiful Dark Twisted Fantasy, were working on a remix to Biebler's song "Runaway Love," I knew Biebler himself probably didn't have shit to do with it. In that sense, it was hardly any different from bum producers on Soundcloud trying to make it seem like they work with famous rappers. Even the idea for remixing a Biebler song he probably jacked from El-P, who dropped a remix of Biebler's "Baby" earlier that summer.

Kanye has long been suspected of stealing ideas from underground rappers. On 7L & Esoteric's 1212, which came out around the same time as My Beautiful Dark Twisted Fantasy, Esoteric accuses Kanye of ripping off the electro-influenced sound of 2006's A New Dope. Kanye comes in for a lot more abuse on the album The Unholy Terror, by Army of the Pharoahs, an underground super group (if you will) featuring Esoteric, in which he's dissed on seemingly every other song and also called a faggot – but not, I should note, by Esoteric, who, childish though he may be, generally leaves the homophobia to Vinnie Paz, et al.

Kanye recorded more songs than he needed for My Beautiful Dark Twisted Fantasy while he was out in Hawaii. Some of them were released as part of a special edition of the album you could probably only get from sites that are an especially bad ripoff, like iTunes, and some of them were released for free via the Internets as part of the kind of weekly free mp3 promotion pioneered in the mid to late '00s by bum rappers like Crooked I and Freeway. The latter was called G.O.O.D. Fridays.

G.O.O.D. Fridays ended up being canceled once Kanye realized that anyone interested enough in hearing leftovers from a Kanye album that they'd stay on the Internets for any longer than they absolutely had to on a Friday afternoon had probably already heard them six months before. Unbeknownst to Kanye, the songs he was releasing each Friday had already been circulating the Internets.

Apparently, haXors were able to break into Hype Williams' computer and steal the entire album. Some of the files that circulated included screencaps the haXors took of Hype Williams' desktop, I guess to let people know where it came from and to brag that they broke into Hype Williams' computer. Hype likes to have an album months before he starts filming a video, so he can listen to it on repeat and figure out which fish eye lenses to use. The process is not as haphazard as you'd think.

It took Kanye a while to realize what was going on. It wasn't until the song he did with the guy from Bon Iver started circulating on some of the white music blogs he checks. A few hip-hop bloggers claimed to have had it for months, but they knew better than to run with it. This was maybe a month before OnSmash was seized by the Department of Homeland Security. Lyor Cohen or someone had probably put them on notice. Anything you can download for free from an NMC blog is, by definition, something a major label couldn't charge money for if they wanted to.

For all of the time, effort and aggravation invested in making My Beautiful Dark Twisted Fantasy the album that got Kanye's career back in order, it ended up selling upwards of half a million copies less than 808s & Heartbreak, which itself sold a million copies less than Graduation – this despite a glowing critical reception even by Kanye standards. My Beautiful Dark Twisted Fantasy might honestly be the most well-reviewed album there ever was. The only thing you can compare it to is Kid A, and someone must not have liked Kid A.

Thus began the current phase of Kanye's career, as of this writing, in which it seems like he has to work twice as hard to get half the results. He's arguably as famous as he ever has been, and yet it seems like interest in his music is at an all time low, though of course still very high in the grand scheme of things.

With his marriage to Kim Kardashian, he seems to have accomplished what he set out to do by baiting Justin Bieber on Twitter, not to mention any benefit derived from reenacting the scene from Kim K Superstar in which Ray J sticks his tongue down Kim Kardashian's throat from behind whilst balls deep inside of her, which I'm sure never gets old... but he must realize, on a certain level, that plenty of other guys have done the exact same thing, and they don't even have an album out, which raises the question of why he even bothers. That would explain the forlorn expression he has on his face most of the time when you see him in public.

12

Ray J Hit It First

Kim Kardashian may have moved on to rappers and ball players, but we all know Ray J hit it first – it's depicted in a film.

The pron film in which Kim Kardashian stars with Brandy's little brother Ray J must be one of the top-selling pron films of all time, of ALL TIME, if the wedding gift that Ray J gave Kim and Kanye is any indication.

Ray J sent the newlyweds a check for $47,000, representing four months worth of royalties he received from the film in 2014. Extrapolated out over the course of this year that means he's still making approximately $140,000 a year from a film that came out in 2007.

A few things to consider:

1) Presumably, Ray J was making way more than that back when Kim K Superstar was the talk of the entire Internets. Who would even buy a copy of Kim K Superstar in 2014? Is it not as easy to illegally download as it was in 2007?

2) If Ray J is making that much from the film, Kim Kardashian must be making way more. The girls in pron films always make way more than the guys. I'd say that has to be the case here. As thoroughly as Ray J worked Kim Kardashian over in Kim K Superstar, I don't know that anyone would buy something just because Ray J was involved.

I couldn't find any exact figures on how much money Kim K Superstar has made over the years in the world's most accurate encyclopedia, which is as much effort as I'm willing to put forth. And the fact of the matter is that you can't trust financial information on pron films anyway.

Back before the pron industry was destroyed by the Internets, pronographers were notorious for exaggerating how much money they were making. To hear pronographers tell it, they were making more money than the regular film industry, Apple Computer and Exxon Mobil combined. I know that a woman's ass is the most valuable commodity in the world, and I'm not arguing that it shouldn't be (fuck a Apple product), but come on.

Now that pron is available for free via the Internets and so much easier to access than actual useful information – which remains scarce, if it exists at all – I suspect that pronographers are exaggerating how much money they're losing. They're probably still making money out the ass. People are willing to pay a dollar for a bottle of water, which is free from the tap – and water sucks balls. Pronography is video of girls sucking balls. It's the best thing ever.

The moment you can't make a dollar from pron is the moment when we've really got a problem, as a society.

A few years ago, when Charlie Sheen went off his meds and declared that he was #biwinning, he was the highest paid actor in all of television. He was getting paid $2 million per episode to appear on Two and a Half Men. TV sitcoms tape 22 episodes per year, so he was making $44 million. In that same period, Kim Kardashian was reportedly making $50 million per year, i.e. higher than any actual actor. It was never reported how much of that was royalties from Kim K Superstar.

Before Kim K Superstar, Kim Kardashian was just another celebutante, albeit maybe the one you'd most like to motorboat. She was friends with Paris Hilton, who was the queen of the celebutantes back in the early 2000s, and her father was Robert Kardashian, part of OJ Simpson's Dream Team. Her family specializes in getting black guys off.

Recently, to commemorate the 20th anniversary of the low-speed chase in the white Bronco that kicked off the OJ trial, the best thing that ever happened, Vanity Fair dug up photos of Kim Kardashian's family on vacation with OJ's family in 1994, a mere matter of months before Nicole Brown Simpson was murdered by Mexican drug dealers and the LAPD tried to frame OJ for it.

Kim Kardashian was built even back then. She's the same age as me, so she couldn't have been any older than about 13, but she had the body of a grown-ass woman. If OJ hadn't been falsely accused of murder, she might have one day caught his eye. It's rumored that OJ is the real father of Kim Kardashian's younger sister Khloe, who stands a good foot taller than the rest of her sisters and has a stocky, NFL-ready build.

Fate may have led Kim Kardashian to spend the early 2000s – the Paris Hilton weed carrier years – married to some black guy no one ever heard of. The wiki says he's a music producer, but that's like saying a young black man is a potential suspect: it tells me nothing at all about the guy. They were married from 2000 to 2004. Kim K Superstar is said to have been filmed in 2003. He filed for divorce from her in 2003, so you do the math – though she would later claim that he put a shoe on her.

There's two sides to every story.

Vivid released Kim K Superstar in early 2007, and that's what kicked off $50 million a year for no apparent reason Kim Kardashian. It was only after the sex tape blew up that E! approached her about doing Keeping Up with the Kardashians. Now her whole family is famous. Khloe Kardashian was married to Lamar Odom for a hot minute, until he all of a sudden became a crackhead. Now French Montana is hitting that. Mom Kris Kardashian had an afternoon TV talk show for a season or two.

Kanye was forced to appear on it to discuss his impending nuptials. He looked like he may have been on Thorazine. Thorazine is the shit Mike Tyson was on when he was on 20/20 with Robin Givens, sitting there looking like a lost child while Givens explained to Baba Wawa how Mike used to choke her out, setting him up to take him to the damn cleaners. It wouldn't be the first time that a celebutante drugged a black athlete before a TV appearance, is what I'm saying. They may be working from a playbook.

How is it that Lamar Odom got with Khloe Kardashian and went so quickly from being a seemingly chill bro to being the Tyrone Biggums of the NBA? He'd already been in the NBA for a minute, at that point. If he had innate crackhead tendencies, they would have already come out. We would have heard about him trying to get a job at Circuit City during the off-season. Mike Tyson is also known to have a bad coke problem. I wonder if that's a side effect of the tranquilizer. Maybe you gotta sniff a little coke to snap out of that daze.

Around the same time that Khloe Kardashian got with Lamar Odom, Kim Kardashian got with some large Halfrican American brother, Kris Humphries. He may have been targeted because he's from Minnesota and he appears to be only slightly more black than she is. He wasn't sophisticated enough to realize that he was being used as a prop on Keeping Up with the Kardashians. With his money, he could have very easily been scoring with chicks hotter than Kim Kardashian. If you follow enough hot chicks on Twitter, you can watch these arrangements unfold in real time.

Their wedding was more hyped than Prince Charles and Lady Di's wedding and Obama's '09 inauguration combined. That shit was all over TV, magazines and the Internets. Kim and Kris Kardashian probably sold off the rights to photos and what have you for a small fortune. Even the wedding ring was employed as propaganda for DeBeers, as was the ring Kanye gave her a few years later. 72 days later Kim Kardashian was in court filing for divorce from Kris Humphries, and even that became a media spectacle from which she probably profited.

Kanye West was said to have been longtime friends with Kim Kardashian before they started dating, shortly after Kris Humphries was dismissed from the set of Keeping Up with the Kardashians. I took this to mean that Kanye had hit that at some point during the 2000s. Possibly on several occasions. Otherwise I'm not sure what it would mean for a guy to be friends with Kim Kardashian. Did they go shopping for velour jogging suits together and exchange theories about the OJ trial? Girls who aren't at risk of getting their shit set out on the curb don't really need guy friends.

I'm not saying it's impossible for a man and a woman to have a platonic relationship. As a marginally famous blogger and now author, I get girls emailing me whom I'll humor – though if I knew these chicks IRL and they just out and out refused to have sex with me, that would be the end of our relationship. There's a plausible deniability element to relationships with girls who aren't in your physical proximity. This was the basis of Brian Johnson's relationship with the girl he scored with in Niagara Falls. She lives in Canada, you wouldn't know her.

I think it goes without saying that if a girl is known for having sex with black guys, and you're a black guy, if the two of you are friends, that means she let you hit that. In mathematics, this is known as the principle of transitivity. If she didn't let you hit that, not only should you not be friends with her, but I wouldn't trust her. That would suggest to me a level of disrespect that can be dangerous. Ask Gary Coleman. Oh yeah, that's right. You can't.

Whenever Kanye hit that, it had to have been after 2003. That's when Kim K Superstar was supposedly shot, and Ray J is adamant that he hit it first to the point where he's written a song about it. If Kanye had evidence to the contrary, I'm sure we would have heard about it by now.

Kanye had yet to release an album, in 2003, but he had several beats on The Blueprint, one of the most famous rap albums of all time, of ALL TIME, and he'd been landing placements on major label releases since the late '90s. Kim Kardashian married that other black guy in 2000, and he's never produced a song anyone ever heard of. She let Ray J work her over like he just got out of jail, and he'll never make a worthwhile contribution to society. Well, if you don't count Kim K Superstar.

Pam Anderson had the OG celebrity sex tape, back in the mid to late '90s, when she was about something. She was huge back then, both literally and figuratively. She had a TV series, films, best-selling magazine covers and what have you, all on the basis of having a ginormous rack – and it wasn't even hers! Any ol' trollop with a few thousand dollars could have gotten ridonkulously large breast implants and become a minor celebrity back then, and in fact many of them did.

Of course this was before Internets technology had evolved to the point where it is now, with smartphones, social media and what have you. Women with truly good bodies are still very rare, arguably even more so than in the past, but with tools like Reddit, Tumblr, Twitter and Instagram, it's easier than ever to – as George W. Bush would say – smoke them out of their holes. I keep a list of the girls with the best racks in the world, and believe me, it's impressive. As Mitt Romney would say, I have binders full of women.

As the story goes, this sex tape, filmed on their honeymoon down in Mexico or somewhere, disappeared from their house either when they were both too high to keep an eye on their sex tape, or when they had some tweakers over to fix a plumbing or electrical issue. (People who do that kind of work, at least here in the Midwest, are always tweakers. I heard they get paid well though.) If they knew when it was stolen, they might have been able to figure out who had it and try to get it back before it was sold to an Internets pron company.

The Pam and Tommy Lee sex tape might be the one celebrity sex tape where I can kinda believe that it really was something that they made "for their own personal amusement," to commemorate their white trash honeymoon, and a drug addict stole it and sold it to a pron company, both because it's such a terrible pron film and because I doubt that they needed the money. Lest we forget, this was back during the late Clinton-era height of close to 0% unemployment, $0.79 a gallon gasoline, record budget surpluses and what have you.

All pron films are terrible. Even my absolute favorite pron films, the ones I've returned to over and over again over the course of my adulthood (don't front like you don't keep a similar cache) are at least morally bad, if not poorly filmed as well. Best case scenario, there's a few minutes that are really, really good. But in a scene that lasts half an hour (which you've still yet to see the very end of), there might be a good 20 minutes worth of shit where you wonder why anyone would want to watch this.

That's because pron films have to make all kinds of concessions, both to the marketplace and to the preferences of the creepy guys who keep pron film companies in business. (I got all my shit "on the arm," as they say in the Italian community.) If it's a film about girls with ginormous asses, for example, they have to keep the girl's ass in pretty much every shot. Which is tragic, if the girl also happens to have pretty good cans.

If it's a hardcore film, there has to be insertion – known in the industry as "the hardcore" – in every shot, during the actual act. Otherwise it's not legit hardcore, and it shouldn't be sold alongside films where there's more of an emphasis on the mechanical aspect of sex. Granted, this has become a moot point, in a time when most pron films are consumed on tube sites like XVideos and Premium Pete's favorite XNXX.

It's a common misconception that people in softcore pron films, like they show on Skinemax, aren't really having sex, but in fact oftentimes they are. They just don't show the penetration, because it's not allowed on the pay cable networks, even though that shit costs an arm and a leg. It's cut out of even those gross Real Sex specials, something I picked up on when I was like middle school-age, because I had such a precocious intellect.

In the Pam Anderson pron film, you don't get much in the way of insertion or a good look at Pam's cans. You might remember seeing clips of it on Entertainment Tonight in which Tommy had the camera trained on his own face, striking Derek Zoolander poses, while he was doing whatever he was doing to Pam Anderson down below, where the camera should have been pointed. They didn't select those clips because they thought they were the best representation of the film, or because that was the only clean bit they could show. That's pretty much all the film was.

You do get a few good shots of Tommy's peen (nullus), probably for no other reason than for Tommy to show off the size of his peen, not unlike that scene in The Brown Bunny in which Chloe Sevigny blows Vince Gallo for a good 15 minutes. Roger Ebert was so jealous that he was forced to get up and leave, and Roger Ebert didn't even fuxwit white chicks, nor did he walk very well. That was a very difficult thing for him to do.

The modern age of the celebrity sex tape kicked off with Paris Hilton's 1 Night in Paris, way TF back in 2003. (I confirmed the date using a search engine.) Because she's the same age as me, she wasn't even that old – though because she has such an admirably fit body, she probably could have pulled off a decent enough sex tape as recently as 2007.

There's a certain community of guys on the Internets who categorize pron chicks based on the year they were born, mostly for the purpose of trying to find the youngest chicks who are legal to watch. A girl who was born in 1996, for example, would be known as "a 1996," and the group of girls who were born that year, many of whom will debut in pron films over the course of the next year or so, are known as "the 1996s." As I write this, at the end of January 2K14, there's yet to be a prominent 1996.

The 1996s have their work cut out for them, if they're ever gonna compete with the 1995s. It turns out that 1995 was as good a year for births of girls who would eventually end up in pron as it was for rap music – and it was one hell of a year for rap music. That was actually the year I started high school, come to think of it, and now all of a sudden I'm not so sure how I feel about this.

Continuing on...

1 Night in Paris, like many subsequent celebrity sex tapes, was marketed as something that was somehow stolen from Paris Hilton's house, like the Pam Anderson sex tape, and sold to a pron company. In fact, as revealed in Sofia Coppola's The Bling Ring, starring my fantasy girlfriend Emma Watson, Paris Hilton doesn't lock her house; you could just waltz right in and steal some-

thing, if you wanted to. The kids from The Bling Ring stole all kinds of shit from her, and she didn't even notice until they stole her drugs. That's what I call having your priorities in order.

The Paris Hilton sex tape was almost certainly fake though, because there's some other pron-like content tacked on to the part with the fucking, to pad it out to DVD-length, and because it's not like Paris Hilton couldn't afford to block distribution of the film if she wanted to. She didn't need the $27,000 the pron company was dangling in front of her to buy heroin, like Pam and Tommy Lee ("allegedly"). Her whole shtick is based around the fact that she has a shedload of money.

I saw a few minutes of 1 Night in Paris once, years ago, and I didn't find it to be very appealing as a pron film. The one thing I did find interesting is the way Paris' eyes glowed in the dark while Rick Salomon was hitting that. If only there was a way to reproduce that effect that didn't involve filming it with a night vision camera. I need a woman who really does light up like a slot machine and pay off in silver dollars, as a young Jack Nicholson once put it.

I've since seen a viral YouTube clip where a chick holds a flashlight up to her huge surgically enhanced breasts, and they light up like one of those mirror balls, so that's something else for the tech community to consider. Maybe we can somehow put lights inside the woman?

Kim Kardashian came into the game as Paris Hilton's weed carrier and eventually far surpassed Paris Hilton, so it was kind of a Jay-Z-Jaz-O situation, except Paris Hilton was ridonkulously wealthy to begin with, so she didn't have to sweat ending up riding the subway on Christmas day with a plastic grocery bag full of MGD tall boys, looking all depressed, possibly on her way back to the Marcy Projects (not to be confused with the great Marcy Playground, of "Sex and Candy" fame).

I don't want to dip into ethnic stereotypes here, even if they're positive, which can still be harmful (to Asians), but it may have been Kim Kardashian's Arab ingenuity that took her career to that next level, the same quality that once helped her father free OJ Simpson. She saw how Paris Hilton's fame skyrocketed overnight with 1 Night in Paris, along with The Simple Life, which just so happened to come out right around the same time (what a coincidence), and she knew she could do Paris one better, because she has ginormous, seemingly real cans.

If she learned how to not flop around like a dead fish, Kim Kardashian could conceivably make a significant amount of money in real pron. She'd easily be one of the top 10 chicks in the history of Ass Parade, especially when you consider that a lot of the top girls from that site have long since disappeared back into America's trailer parks. And by "a significant amount of money" I mean upwards of $200,000 over the course of her career, pre-any split she's worked out with a guy who has a gold tooth, whose role is to drive her to her scenes in an '89 Cutlass.

So yeah, it may not have been worth her while financially. The idea was just to get her name in the papers. I wonder if she even gets a check from Vivid. If she does, it's probably pales in comparison to what she made them... since it's not like she's gonna have them audited. Imagine if you're Kanye, at the house he bought with Kim Kardashian a while back, going through the mail each month and finding that check from Vivid. On the one hand, I imagine there would be a certain level of pride, but on the other hand it would mostly just cause you to question having a baby by her.

Similarly, I imagine it would be difficult to be out somewhere and hear that song "I Hit It First," about how Ray J had sex with your baby's mother back in '03, before dat ass needed to be photoshopped to the extent that it does now, and even made a famous pron film with her. If I were out somewhere (I know...) and I knew Kanye was in the building, I'd tell the DJ to throw on "I Hit It First," for lulz purposes. "I Hit It First" would definitely be in the jukebox of any joint that I owned, along with the Journey and what have you.

Not only was Kanye's baby's mother in a pron film, she was in a pron film with a guy who's primarily known for being Brandy's little brother. A guy who's sister put him on allowance. Into his 20s, he was living in a kid-size bedroom in her house, drinking straight from the milk carton and then putting it back in the fridge, out of spite over the fact that she was born with (a modicum of) talent and he wasn't. It's a wonder she didn't get an STD on her lips.

I remember I saw Ray J on an episode of MTV Cribs around the time I graduated from college. It wasn't even a Ray J episode of Cribs; it was a Brandy episode. He just happened to be there, because he lived there. Ray J and I are the same age, and the college I went to kept me around for a while, because I was such a good example for the younger students, so you do the math.

In college, I read somewhere on a message board that Ray J was slaying a lot of pussy in LA. Being Brandy's little brother might be the sorriest claim to fame possible, but it's probably perfect for scoring with girls who grew up on the WB, who can't be difficult to score with anyway. Plus, he's got a huge schlong, and once word gets out that a guy has a huge schlong, chicks will hit him up just to score with a guy who's packing a certain girth. Don't believe for a minute that shit about the motion in the ocean. That's for chicks who haven't been sufficiently stretched out.

You can imagine my surprised then when I saw that Ray J didn't even have his own place. He was scoring with chicks in the kid bedroom at Brandy's house. The allowance she was giving him must not have been enough to both keep him in alcohol and pay the rent on a decent apartment. Bringing chicks back to Brandy's Cribs-worthy house may have been part of the plan, but you'd think the effect would be ruined by then bringing them to the fourth biggest bedroom, across from the linen closet.

Having said that, if these books ever take off (it could happen!), I might get a race car bed, for sex purposes. If you're the kind of girl who would be interested in that sort of thing, and you're at least 18 (preferably as close to 18 as possible), email me.

I wrote about how Ray J was using his status as Brandy's little brother to violate women, and how someone should kill him (which I later learned is technically not legal), and Ray J must have seen it and had my blog removed from the Internets for a few days back in, I think '04. It was an important case in the history of free speech on the Internets, and it might one day be taught in college, even if I have to teach it myself. I wrote all about it in my first book The Mindset of a Champion, for sale now at Amazon.

So Ray J definitely had plenty of experience. It shows, at least to a certain degree, in Kim K Superstar. It's not the best pron film in the world, but he definitely put a beating on that pussy. Whereas Kim Kardashian is probably still spending money from the OJ trial and was only trying to get her name in the paper, Ray J seemed like he may have actually been auditioning to be the stunt schlong in pron films – probably the most coveted job in the world, based on how many guys want to do it. Maybe even more so than the presidency. Think about it.

As is the case with other celebrity pron films, it's not shot very well. Ostensibly, it's just the two of them in the room getting it on, Ray J holding the camera or setting it somewhere nearby. Sometimes you get the sense that there's a third party operating the camera, but it's hard to tell. There's some penetration shots, but I don't know that there's anything that counts as a true penetration shot, in the sense that you can see the actual opening to Kim Kardashian's vagina.

You don't get a very good look at her cans either. They show up all of about twice, I guess so that too many people didn't angrily return the DVD to Adam and Eve. (What an awkward trip to the post office that would be.) It doesn't make sense to me, since you get a full-on look at them, from a few different angles, in an issue of Playboy. It's not like there's anything wrong with them, aside from perhaps some age-related sag. I'm actually in the same issue, in an article about whether or not black people should own guns.

It's funny how Kanye's career continues to intersect with my own. I can only assume that this is fate and hope that it translates into book sales. (Another weird coincidence I just found out via the wiki, since we're on the topic: The guy who was in the Paris Hilton sex tape was married to Pam Anderson. No word on if they have a sex tape. They have to though, right?)

Kim Kardashian and Ray J seem to be working from a shot list, possibly supplied to them by someone from Vivid, lest the whole thing end up being backshots – which would have been perfect for me personally. The lighting is decent enough in the wide-angle shots, but it gets kinda grainy in some of the medium-length shots, focused primarily on Ray J's schlong, like the room light may have been obscured by the covers on the bed.

I should note that the version I saw, which I reviewed for XXL back in '07, was the one they were giving away for free at World Star. I think they had both the video streaming and a download link, but it looked like they were forced to get rid of the streaming video. The download link still worked, which is how I got it. Mind you, this was seven years ago. If you tried it now, if you could even find it, your computer would probably explode. I'd suggest finding a streaming version at any number of tube sites, which can easily be downloaded via browser extension.

The World Star version is about 40 minutes long with an ad at the end touting an even longer version with better-quality video. They showed a few clips, cut up in a sort of mini trailer, but they looked like the exact same thing as the film I just saw. Unless there's a money shot, I wouldn't bother trying to dig for it. If there were a money shot, I'd actually pay money for pron for the first time in my adult life. Er, I'd try to save up.

13

Yeezus H. Tapdancing Christ

Making money in the entertainment industry is mostly just a matter of getting your name in the paper. The more often you're mentioned in the media, the more albums, tickets and what have you you can sell, and the more you can charge to perform.

It doesn't matter so much what you do to get your name in the paper. You could get a lot of press for recording one of the best albums in years, supposedly, like Kendrick "Hobbit Hands" Lamar did a couple of years ago, but what if you only had one really good idea, and you already used it 10 years ago? That's no reason why you shouldn't continue to pursue a career as a recording artist.

If you're a woman, and you've got a decent enough ass, you can have it photographed on the reg, and you can flip that fame into having your own perfume from which you make millions of dollars per year. I don't know for a fact that Kim Kardashian has her own perfume, but I do happen to know – from having to work behind a perfume counter for a while, a while back (I really am putting too much information in this book) – that Paris Hilton, on whom Kim Kardashian based her career, has her own perfume.

Paris Hilton's perfume, Heiress, continued to sell pretty well even after she began to fade back into obscurity, where she belongs, either because people actually liked how it smells, or because this was the semi-rural Midwest, where people are about five years behind the times. But I don't know if a Kim Kardashian perfume would be as successful, because it could be a situation like the Michael Jordan cologne from back in the early '90s, where it actually doesn't smell half-bad, but it seems like it would, based on the name. Does it actually smell like Michael Jordan during a game?

Kim Kardashian is part-Armenian and part-CAC and was raised in the rich, white part of LA. She's essentially a white person. But she has a ginormous ass that might be impossible to reach with her relatively short arms, and a swarthy complexion like someone from the Middle East or North Africa. Sometimes you meet people from Africa, especially if they've got that kinte cloth shower curtain thing on instead of regular clothes, and they smell like ass. It's not (necessarily) because it's been that long since they washed their ass, it's because they don't believe in wearing deodorant in that part of the world. They think deodorant stinks.

Paris Hilton's career only ever went but so far, because she has a body like a pre-pubescent boy. I always thought she was kinda hot, but no one who read my blog ever agreed with me. A girl like that might be really hot when you see her in person, but that kind of hotness can be difficult to capture in a photograph on the Internets. You need either a ginormous ass or ginormous cans in order to make it "pop" visually, as my personal stylist at Men's Wearhouse would say. (I carry his business card in my wallet, in case of a fashion emergency.)

It's one of the flaws of the technology, not unlike how the film you use in a camera was purposely designed to not photograph black women's skin very well, and that's one of the main reasons black women aren't considered as desirable as white women. I read that on Black People Twitter, but it seems like it must be true, right? There isn't always a strong correlation between the most popular girls on the Internets and the most objectively attractive girls. Depending on what kind of site it is, a girl's face might not even matter as much. It's more along the lines of being in a strip club.

Kim Kardashian's ass is wildly mediocre. She's packing a lot of volume, but so are middle-aged black women who drive city buses and wear those gray polyester pants. No one seems to give a shit, I suspect, for a couple of reasons: (1) White people have only really been into chicks with fat asses – to the extent that they are, in fact, into chicks with fat asses – for a few years now. They don't really know what they're talking about. (2) If they're just gonna photoshop the shit out of your pictures anyway, you're better off having more ass, which they can just erase and try to sculpt into something visually appealing.

Anyway, the numbers speak for themselves. Kim Kardashian made enough money last year to land at number 80 on this year's Forbes Celebrity 100, ahead of people who actually do something, including Stephen King, Dr. Phil McGraw and Seth MacFarlane. She was only five spaces below Will Smith. And because the way those Forbes lists are tabulated is some ol' BS, it's likely she made even more money than they're reporting. Their estimate, I notice, doesn't include royalties from Kim K Superstar, possibly on orders from her publicist. She makes enough now that she can make the list, albeit down in the lower reaches, without including her main source of income.

Kanye has been trying to play the same game for the past couple of years now, even going so far as to have a baby with Kim Kardashian. It hasn't been working as well for him business-wise – Yeezus seems to be following the trend of each subsequent album of his selling worse than the one that came before, established way back with the release of Late Registration but really kicking into high gear with 808s & Heartbreak, and he played to half-empty stadiums on the ill-fated Yeezus tour, which was also plagued by accidents and technical mishaps – but it could be worse, for all we know.

We don't know what Kanye's sales would be like at this point if he wasn't acting like a jackass in interviews on the reg, staging fake fights with the paparazzi at the airport every now and again, standing next to Kim Kardashian while her ass is having its picture taken, so on and so forth. It could be worse. I can't imagine it would be any better, because his music has limited appeal to the kind of people who look down on such shenanigans, who seek out music that has real substance – lyrically lyrical rappers, as they're referred to, disparagingly, by cultural tourists.

Really, those kinds of tactics are probably best-suited for up and coming artists. Once you've been around for a certain period of time, you become a known quantity. People already know what your music sounds like, and if they don't want to buy it, they're not gonna buy it, regardless of who your baby's mother is. They're gonna see that you've got a new album coming out, and they're gonna think to themselves, How often do I listen to his last album? This is not 2005, is it?

On the other hand, in the past few years, we've seen several artists go from being entirely unheard of to being fairly well known, at least on the Internets, in quite literally a matter of hours. One day there was no such thing as Lana

Del Rey, unless you count the one album she made before, when she was being marketed as more of a teen slut-pop artist, which I believe was released under a different name, and the next thing you know she was all over the place. A meeting was held between the TIs at Interscope and the top brass at Pitchfork, a fawning review of her song "Video Games" hit the Internets, and the rest, as they say, was history. Shot out to Ian Cohen.

She got a lot of mileage out of think pieces about the fact that she has no indie credibility to speak of, her father is a domain name scammer, and it's impossible to review her music fairly, because she's entirely too hot to say anything bad about. Two years later, I'm still not sure whether or not I like her music. It seems like I shouldn't, for enough reasons to fill a reasonably-priced ebook, but I listen to it, and it doesn't sound half bad to me. Do I actually like it, or has Interscope somehow found a way to use my cell phone to analyze my subconscious? Is that even her singing?

I would never actually listen to her album, but I find myself really liking her videos (quelle surprise), and in fact, I think she's the kind of artist who's best enjoyed via music videos, like Michael Jackson or, uh, a-Ha I guess. In particular, that video with her and A$AP Rocky, where Rocky looks like he's about to "drop a digit" on her, and there's also a reenactment of the Kennedy assassination, might be the one modern music video that's worthy of the pantheon of great early '90s-era videos like REM's "Losing My Religion." She really does have a video like that, right? I'm not just imagining that.

Where would Odd Future be without the think piece-industrial complex? Probably in a sweaty basement somewhere sending out emails talking about how a deposed prince in Africa has $10 million in a hidden bank account, and he needs your personal information in order to have it transferred. They've built an entire cottage industry based on trolling people. People are buying tickets to their shows just to go home and write blog posts about how their constant use of the other f-word is "problematic."

For a minute there, they were being heralded as an actual rap group you'd want to listen to, the modern equivalent of the Wu-Tang Clan, but that didn't last for any longer than it took for people who know from rap music to download one of their mixtapes. The very best member of Odd Future, Earl Sweatshirt, is arguably better than U-God, and that's about it, but U-God is still on way more good songs than Earl Sweatshirt will ever be on. The video for "Cherchez La Ghost" is better than Earl Sweatshirt's entire life, including that stint in Samoa.

The problem with trying to advance your career via trolling is that it might increase your celebrity, but it won't necessarily help you sell very many albums. Those Tyler the Juggalo albums, combined, probably didn't sell as many copies as the last J. Cole album (which also famously outsold Yeezus) did its first week out, and you can't find a single person on the Internets who will openly admit to liking J. Cole. Earl Sweatshirt didn't sell a single album to a person who didn't need one to write a review. They were hoping the SEO traffic would be sufficient to make back what it cost.

Yeezus may have been the most written about Kanye album to date, with all of its talk of shoving a fist in a woman's vagina like the civil rights sign, and eating an Asian woman's pussy with duck sauce, and I'm thinking it may have also sold a few copies to, or was streamed via any number of services now available (for which he would have received quite literally a few pennies), by people who needed to have a listen in order to explain why this kind of content was problematic. Maybe not enough people to sustain a career, but again, what are you gonna do?

In order to boost sales and also harvest people's personal information, a deal was struck in which Google's obscure music download store, which many people probably didn't even realize they had on their phone, gave Yeezus away for free for the last few days of 2013. It was the low expectations equivalent of the deal Jay-Z struck with Samsung to give away [Austin Powers voice] one million copies of the god-awful Magna Carta Holy Grail to people with Samsung Galaxy phones, and it may have been necessary for Def Jam to avoid having to have a difficult meeting with the IRS.

I happened to be on the Internets that week, because I don't enjoy spending time with family and friends, and I figured what the fuck. I was planning on writing this book during the summer of 2K14 (it got pushed up some, because the subject matter of the book I was working on was unsavory, even by my own admittedly low standards, and I began to have second thoughts about it), not unlike how I wrote NaS Lost in the summer of 2K13, and I haven't heard a Kanye album since 2005, damn near a decade ago. (Jesus.) The price was definitely right.

I also picked up The Bones of What You Believe by Chvrches. It sorta kinda reminds me of the OMD song from Pretty in Pink, which of course touches a sensitive brother like me emotionally. Nullus. But so does Summer = Youth by M83, which I like even more.

Yeezus is a sparsely written album, lyrically, either because Kanye has limited ability to write lyrics, because he's not a real MC, and he's never been particularly adept at expressing himself verbally, as evidenced by the incident at the Hurricane Katrina telethon, or because he intended for it to be that way stylistically. I actually think it's the latter, and I only suggested that it might be because he's a crap lyricist because, as Angie Varona once said on ABC's Nightline, I need to take my life off the Internets.

After all, he could just pay people to write his lyrics, like he always does. He seems to be channeling the even more inarticulate Chief Keef, who's credited as a songwriter on Yeezus, along with – no hyperbole – 66 other people. Only as many people as were necessary to craft such a deeply personal statement, and not a single person more. This is not some three-disc No Limit compilation he's putting together. In fact, those albums may have had less songwriters than Yeezus. (Really, they didn't have any songwriters.) Lest we forget, Yeezus only has 10 songs.

Kanye doesn't discuss how it feels to have a career that's falling apart, a new white accent, and a baby by a woman who was once in a pron film with Ray J, let alone the problems he's been having trying to get European designers to cut him a check to create a line of leather jogging pants, so much as he just kinda sounds angry and makes a lot of allusions to having sex with white women, both as a form of revenge and "for his own personal amusement."

When he paid whoever it was to write that line about how he's got black dick all in your spouse again, who got more dreaded n-words off than Johnnie Cochran, he must have drawn the connection between the OJ trial and his baby's mother, right? He's dense, but he's not that dense. I think I even once said that Kim Kardashian got more black men off than Johnnie Cochran, back when she was dating Reggie Bush, and that may have been where Kanye got it from. I could sue and demand to be listed as the 68th songwriter on Yeezus, but sometimes it's important to be the bigger man, both literally and figuratively. Plus, there's no way it'll ever recoup.

In the song, Kanye's talking about having sex with some guy's wife, who's had sex with a lot of black guys. No white woman in America today is as well-known for having sex with black guys as Kim Kardashian. She's the pop culture equivalent of that one girl you went to school with who all of a sudden developed a blaccent in the 8th grade. By the 10th grade she had a half-black baby. It supposedly belonged to one black kid in your class, but it looked like another black kid in your class, and really it could have belonged to any number of people.

Kim Kardashian's father Robert Kardashian was also part of the team that got OJ Simpson off (no Boutros), and it can be said that pretty much her entire family is in the business of getting black men off in some form or another. If the Kardashians had a family crest, at least one panel would consist of a picture of a black man with that same look of deep satisfaction on his face that OJ had when the verdict was read. Her two younger sisters, Kendall and Kylie, probably don't appeal to any black men other than myself, but then they aren't Kardashians, now are they? Having said that, they shouldn't let that keep them from entering into the family business, so to speak. Daddy like…

Speaking of no one's looking!

What I took from this is that Kanye, on a certain level, resents Kim Kardashian, probably in part due to the fact that she had quite a bit of mileage by the time he got to her, and not just any mileage, but Ray J mileage (her vagine has probably never been as tight as he would like), and in part because the main reason he's with her, when he could have sex with an entire family of women with a weird-looking tank ass for what he pays for a pair of leather jogging pants, is to get his name in the paper, and he resents that that's what his career has come to. He's got a baby by the town bicycle, and he's paying 67 people to write his rhymes, on an album that ended up being outsold by J. Cole. This is not how it was supposed to work out.

Something in Kanye's brain seemed to snap all of a sudden in late 2014. He's always been a little bit off, but the lukewarm reception to Yeezus, combined with the problems he's been having with his fashion career and the concerns one might have with being married to Kim Kardashian must have somehow combined to drive him completely over the edge.

In an interview with some guy named Zane Lowe from the BBC, Kanye went so far as to compare himself to Steve Jobs and also complained that Fendi wouldn't allow him to design a pair of leather jogging pants. This was crazy crackhead talk. Crackheads love sweatpants (and sometimes the combination of sweatpants and dress shoes). DJ AM's dead body was found in a pair of sweatpants. Ask Paul Rosenberg.

The whole thing ran over an hour long, and I wasn't about to watch, both because there's only but so much time in a day and also because I'm still using a computer I bought back when I was with XXL, and I don't know if it's capable of playing an hour-long YouTube video. It might melt down. This is less of an issue with the pron I watch (for research purposes), because I can just skip to the really good parts. I get more work done that way. #productivity

I'm only familiar with the parts about how Kanye is the equivalent of Steve Jobs and the leather jogging pants because they became part of a sketch on Jimmy Kimmel Live! in which kids reenact the interview while drinking milkshakes. As far as I know, the dialogue in the sketch is straight from the interview. I think that's the point of the sketch, actually: having kids read it heightens the ridiculous nature of the dialogue. But what do I know? I'm no expert on comedy. I might have to ask one of these people who type jokes into Twitter all day.

Speaking of which, the next day on Twitter Kanye went off on Kimmel. Someone must have sent him a link to the video of the kids reenacting his Zane Lowe interview. In a series of ALL CAPS tweets, Kanye told Kimmel that he was having problems with people climbing over his fence to try to take pictures of his daughter, and that it would be impossible for Kimmel to put himself in Kanye's shoes because he doesn't get enough pussy, because there's something wrong with his face.

Then I guess Jimmy Kimmel called Kanye, trying to pursue back channels, which is standard operating procedure in corporate media disputes (ask Peter Rosenberg), and Kanye reminded Kimmel that he'd attended Kimmel's family's wedding, whatever that means. Kimmel explained to Kanye that that wasn't any of his family, just someone he was friends with, which Kanye took as further proof of Kimmel's manipulative nature. Kanye probably only attended the wedding because he thought it was one of Kimmel's relatives and he was trying to score brownie points.

Why would a man voluntarily elect to attend a wedding of someone he doesn't even know? I don't even like attending my own relatives' weddings. The only reason I can think of is to try to score. Single girls at weddings will fuck literally anything that moves – they're like George W. Bush. But that's a moot point, because Kanye has a shedload of money. He could hit up any ol' random hot chick on Twitter and order her to come have sex with him for free.

Kanye elaborated on the problems he's had trying to convince European fashion designers to let him design a pair of leather jogging pants in an interview with Sway on Sirius satellite radio. This was one of the most breathtaking bits of audio to ever hit the Internets, right up there with that recording of Young Buck crying on the phone with 50 Cent. Disrespect has rarely been as palpable as when Kanye told Sway that his clothing line isn't Ralph, no one ever heard of it, and therefore he doesn't have the answers.

It's a testament to Sway's magnanimity that he didn't just go upside Kanye's head, and presumably that's why he's the only black guy to work at MTV for more than like three years, outlasting the likes of Combat Jack and the guys who used to do those hip-hop roundtables, explaining why [insert name of corporate rapper du jour] deserved to be on this year's list of the 10 hottest MCs in the game. Imagine having to compromise yourself in that way just to make a living, only to end up doing a podcast a few years later. In a round about way, this may have been what Kanye was getting at.

Kanye could have put himself on time out, to regroup, except he had to go on tour behind Yeezus that winter. He probably spent a shedload of money recording that album, and given how few people bought it, that was the only way he was gonna at least break even. That's why getting some kind of clothing line off the ground was becoming increasingly important. If he's paying such a lengthy-ass list of people to write his songs for him, and then he's going out on tour with all kinds of expensive props and lighting, how is he supposed to make any money?

The tour kicked off in New York, where Kanye appeared on Power 105's The Breakfast Club with Angela Yee, DJ Envy and Charlamagne Tha God. Presented with a clearly unstable Kanye and hence sensing an opportunity for radio gold, Charlamagne Tha God et al. baited Kanye into yet another discussion of leather jogging pants, Kanye's alleged creative genius and the problems he's had dealing with these corporations. This time, Kanye made the mistake of bringing the Jews into it. According to Kanye, black people don't have the same connections as Jews, and that's why Obama hasn't been able to push through reforms.

Wait, what?

The fact of the matter is that black people really don't have the connections that Jews have, and that's one of the many, many reasons black people can't get ahead; and while it's not anti-Semitic for a black guy to point that out, it is racist for a Jew to suggest that it is. But I'm actually less concerned with the substance of what Kanye said than the fact that he brought up the Jews in the first place. What he said may not have been anti-Semitic, but the non sequitir way in which he mentioned it was, at best, a little bit off. Though there probably isn't an ideal way to invoke the Jews in a discussion of your own business problems. LOL

Kanye also made thinly veiled reference to the problems Arsenio Hall had with the Jews back in the mid '90s, elsewhere in the interview. Specifically, he said that if he "turned up" too much in interviews, people would stop buying his albums, and he'd be out of a job, like Arsenio, with the subtext being that Arsenio lost his show after he ran afoul of the Jews by booking an interview with "Calypso" Louis Farrakhan and then giving him pretty much an entire show to spout his views, which Jews don't particularly care for. If memory serves correctly, he was off the air like two weeks later.

20 years later, Arsenio was on either Dancing with the Stars or The Apprentice, or possibly both. His appearances went well, he didn't say any off brand shit about the Jews and so CBS gave him own show back... which ended up lasting for less than a year this time, but not because of anything he said; people just didn't give a shit. Backstage at the Grammys, where he was a presenter, a reporter asked Arsenio about what Kanye said about him, prompting Arsenio to go off. His new show was already on its way off the air at that point, and I'm sure the last thing he needed was Kanye reminding people about that Farrakhan shit.

Once the Yeezus tour made its way to the real heart of Murica, where people like Bol live, it didn't fare very well at all. We don't have $40 to go see a concert, and if we did, we'd want to spend it on someone who can actually sing. Personally, I don't recommend paying money to watch someone rap. That's just giving money away. Kanye ended up selling 4,500 tickets to a venue that holds over 18,000 people, in Kansas City, on the other end of my native Missouri. The tour had already been postponed a few weeks, supposedly due to an issue with a lighting rig. Likely story.

Then it was announced that Kanye signed a deal with Adidas. He'd been working with Nike since at least as far back as when he did that song with Rick Rubin, DJ Premier, KRS-One and whoever else got a check behind that shillery, and he'd put out at least two pairs of shoes that I'm pretty sure were based on the shoes from the second Back to the Future movie that lace themselves. But these don't actually lace themselves, I don't think.

Kanye says Nike was taking entirely too long to actually pay him for those Back to the Future shoes. Also, he didn't have a real deal with them, like an athlete, where he would receive a percentage of each shoe sold. He just received a one-time fee to use his name on a pair of shoes. I'm pretty sure Dinosaur Jr. had the same deal back in the late '90s, so it couldn't have been very lucrative. And that might be why he hasn't received another check: he's not entitled to another check. Has Kanye been calling Nike demanding money he's not rightly owed? This is another thing crackheads do. I've worked in customer service.

A few days later, I saw on Twitter that Drake had signed with Nike to release his own Air Jordan. It just looked like a regular Air Jordan with gold glitter all over it, like something Liberace would wear to play basketball against Scott Thorson, or if they played two on two against Sigfried and Roy. Game, blouses... which in that case I guess would mean that everyone won. No homo.

Nike is a gozillion dollar company that spends boatloads of money on marketing each year. The shoes only cost like eight dollars a pair to make, so any perceived value that they might have has merely been implanted in your head by advertising. I say all this to say that (a) I still fuxwit No Logo 15 years after the fact, and (b) I don't think that Nike would announce that they signed Drake a mere matter of days after Kanye West was all over the Internets bitching and moaning about how he'd been treated by them unless they purposely intended to. They pay attention to these things.

This was a changing of the guard. Nike was declaring that Drake is the new

Kanye West, and Kanye West is the new Bobby Brown. Bobby Brown used to be married to Whitney Houston, who had sex with Ray J (who didn't?), so you can see how this is all related. Kanye is becoming increasingly crack-ish. Bobby Brown is rumored to have been on crack. Drake sells more albums now than Kanye, and his popularity is still increasing. Kanye's career has been in decline for years. This analogy honestly could be worse.

More importantly, Drake is with "the program," meaning that he knows better than to go on the Internets talking about whether or not he got paid on time. Drake is famously signed to a dreaded n-word who's signed to a dreaded n-word who's signed to another dreaded n-word. Word on the street is that he's yet to receive so much as a dollar in royalties from Cash Money. And yet he consistently denies rumors that he's thinking about bolting the ironically-named Cash Money for a label where you actually get paid. Even if he wanted to, I doubt he has the balls to demand a meeting with that guy who looks like the black Lurch from The Addams Family. He'll be on Cash Money forever.

But I doubt he's hurting for money. I've seen pictures of a house he owns in LA, on TMZ or somewhere, that looks like some sort of fancy resort for rich gay couples. He paid $9 million for it. I also saw where he was selling a place he owns in Canada for about half that. He must have a deal with the various other companies he works with where his checks aren't sent to Cash Money's offices, where they could be "intercepted." It's the same concept as UPS not delivering packages to neighborhoods with a certain percentage of black people. With this system in place, and with his unwillingness to rock the boat, as they used to say back in the 1970s, Drake seems poised to be the true heir to Jay-Z that Kanye once could have been.

Kanye, meanwhile, seems poised to follow in the footsteps of Jay's fellow Rocafella Records co-founder Damon Dash, who, once supposedly worth $200 million, has since been reduced to sleeping on people's couches in Brooklyn and baiting white rap label execs via Instagram. Dame blames Lyor Cohen for the dissolution of Rocafella Records, and he seems to be upset that Joie Manda could even have a high profile job in the music industry, let alone one of the top positions at Interscope, which he took after walking away from the top position at Def Jam. Joie Manda is the guy who used to bring Funkmaster

Flex his scarves and water, for when his throat got parched and his brow got sweaty. Irv Gotti was instrumental in bringing Jay-Z, DMX and Ja Rule to Def Jam. Irv Gotti actively campaigned for the top job at Def Jam. Joie Manda was the one who got it.

To hear Dame Dash tell it, this is because companies like Universal Music, the company that owns Def Jam and like half the music business, are run by culture vultures – people who don't come from within hip-hop, who live to exploit hip-hop. I'm sure there's at least some truth to that, and I'd like for there to be some truth to that anyway, because I find that sort of thing amusing, but I wonder if this is not really just a matter of labels not wanting to work with people who lack the sense god gave geese. Irv Gotti probably ruined his chances of working for Def Jam again when the FBI raided the building looking for evidence that he was laundering drug money for Kenneth "Supreme" McGriff. Remember the scene in that Hard Knock Life tour documentary where Dame was barking on someone from Def Jam about the tour jackets? Of course they're not gonna make him president.

I could run down the list of reasons why no one would want to make a sizable investment in a Kanye-led venture, despite the amount of money he's generated for the entertainment industry over the past 10 years or so, but then I already have over the course of this book. 10 years ago, Kanye was putting the president on notice on live TV, and now here he is on the radio talking about how the Jews secretly run the government. He's been involved in all kinds of crazy shit in the interim. Who knows what he'll do next. The same thing that makes him such a compelling artist is precisely the reason why he can't talk anyone into going into business with him.

If worst comes to worst, I've got an idea for how he can make some money. This is something involving both him and his baby's mother…

ABOUT THE AUTHOR

BYRON CRAWFORD is the founder and editor of the legendary hip-hop blog ByronCrawford.com: The Mindset of a Champion and a former columnist for XXL magazine. He lives in a shanty town.

CPSIA information can be obtained at www.ICGtesting.com
Printed in the USA
LVOW09s0530010914

401796LV00012BA/229/P

9 781500 586188